good green HOMES

good green HOMES

JENNIFER ROBERTS

Gibbs Smith, Publisher
Salt Lake City

First Edition
07 06 05 04   5 4 3

Published by
Gibbs Smith, Publisher
P.O. Box 667
Layton, Utah 84041

Orders: (1-800) 748-5439
www.gibbs-smith.com

Editorial director: Suzanne Gibbs Taylor
Designed by Dawn DeVries Sokol
Printed and bound in Hong Kong

Library of Congress Cataloging-in-Publication Data

Roberts, Jennifer, 1962–
  Good green homes : creating better homes for a healthier planet /
Jennifer Roberts.—1st ed.
        p. cm.
  ISBN 1-58685-179-9
  1. Architecture—Environmental aspects. 2. Architecture, Domestic.
I. Title.
NA2542.35.R63 2003
728'.37—dc21

                                                    2003007570

CONTENTS

Use the Right Stuff

Healthy • Recycled • Locally produced
• Durable • Sustainably harvested •
Rapidly renewable • Reclaimed

Afterword: Restoring Our World, One Home at a Time

Building green means using resources wisely. It's also about creating places that inspire us and nurture our spirits.

what's GREEN got to do with it?

Green. It conjures images of a meadow in spring and the color of money. What's green got to do with our homes? In essence, green building—or sustainable building—means being smart about how we use energy, water, and building materials so that we can live well without needlessly damaging the environment. It means building beautiful homes that meet our needs and aspirations while ensuring we leave our world healthy enough so that future generations can meet theirs.

Creating a good green home isn't just about conservation, about using less or saving more—although that's certainly one aspect of it. Creating a good green home is about recognizing that our domestic decisions have repercussions in the larger world. It's about creating vital communities where people from all walks of life help each other thrive. It's about using our ingenuity and spirit to create places that nurture, honor, and celebrate people and the planet.

CREATING A BETTER HOME

American homes built today are—more or less—satisfactory. They're more energy efficient than two decades ago. They meet building codes for health and safety. They have the modern conveniences we've come to expect. But is satisfactory good enough?

Consider these statistics. The air inside our homes can be two to five times more polluted than the air outside, no matter whether we live in an industrial or rural region. Homes account for more than 20 percent of all U.S. energy consumption. Building a 2,000-square-foot home results in more than 25,000 pounds of construction waste.

Today we have a choice. We can keep creating homes that require vast amounts of energy to heat and cool, homes that are built with trees cut from ancient forests, homes that may be filled with materials harmful to our health. Or we can create better homes that are healthier to live in, easier on the environment, more valuable over the long-term, and more delightful to come home to.

The little girl who plays and sleeps here is blissfully unaware that the builder who built her house cared about her comfort and her future. Energy-efficient windows, good insulation, nontoxic paints and interior finishes, and a fresh-air ventilation system contribute to a comfortable and healthy indoor environment.

Here are just some of the direct benefits of good green homes:

More comfortable. A good green home is a more comfortable home. It's carefully built and well insulated so it doesn't overheat in the summer or feel chilly in the winter. Daylight, cross-ventilation, and other low-tech measures help keep spaces naturally and comfortably in tune with our bodies and the outdoors. Efficient lighting, heating, and cooling systems kick in when simpler solutions can't do the job on their own.

Healthier. A good green home has fewer building products and furnishings made from materials that might undermine our health. Good ventilation, provided either by natural or mechanical means, helps keep the air fresh. Daylight brightens the rooms, providing an uplifting atmosphere.

Greater value. A good green home gives you more for your money. Good green homes are built to last, with quality design and construction that hold up over time. They cost less to live in and maintain because they're built to be energy efficient and durable.

These immediate advantages are reason enough to go green. The deeper benefits may be less obvious. Using an energy-efficient lightbulb, for example, saves you money. It also results in less demand for electricity that,

> What we do at home may
> not change the world,
> but it can change a lot.

in turn, results in less pollution from power plants, which may help a child with asthma breathe a little easier. Choosing recycled plastic lumber for your deck will spare you from ever having to spend a Saturday afternoon staining it—and in a broader context it means that somewhere a tree remains standing. What we do at home may not change the world, but it can change a lot.

THE GOOD LIFE, THE GREEN LIFE

If green's so great, why aren't we all living in good green homes?

Perhaps it's because some of us don't yet know that healthier, more sustainable housing exists. Or we know that it's possible to create a different kind of home, but fear it will cost too much. Few of us have made it a priority to demand that the home-building industry offer us better alternatives, so the industry continues to build what they think we want. Some of us may assume we'll have to sacrifice amenities or aesthetics—that we can't live the good life *and* the green life.

If you still associate green-built housing with the unconventional or the quirky—tree houses, geodesic domes, dwellings constructed of tires or Coke bottles—think again. Those kinds of houses represent one portion of the green building spectrum, but for practical, aesthetic, financial, or emotional reasons, most of us wind up living in more conventional dwellings. We may want a house that reminds us of where we grew up (or where we *wish* we had grown up). Perhaps we've fallen in love with Arts & Crafts bungalows or midcentury modern ranches or center-hall Colonials, and so we think we can't have our dream and be green, too.

It doesn't have to be an either/or choice. Good green homes simply mean better homes: homes remodeled or built to save energy and resources, homes that enhance our well-being rather than sap our strength, and homes that honor the natural abundance and beauty that surround us. We don't need to sacrifice affordability, style, or comfort. We can have the good life *and* the green life—maybe not all at once, maybe not without making some mistakes and compromises along the way, but there are steps we can each take that will lead us toward a more environmentally sustainable future.

> We can have the
> good life *and*
> the green life.

Many types of homes can be good green homes, whether they're modern or traditional, in the city, in the suburbs, or in the country. The owners of this new farmhouse in rural Washington State marvel at its low energy use, a result of energy-efficient windows, good daylighting, a wraparound porch for summer shading, and an efficient masonry heater.

INSIDE *GOOD* GREEN *HOMES*

Good Green Homes is for people who believe in the power of one person—or one home—to make a world of difference. It's for homeowners, certainly—people who are considering redecorating or remodeling their home, or buying or building a new home. It's also for home renters, who might be surprised by how much is within their power to change. Even small actions, from using nontoxic household cleaners to setting back the thermostat a few degrees at night, can make a home healthier or reduce energy bills.

Good Green Homes is also for architects, builders, interior designers, and others who may be intrigued or inspired by the homes featured here. While this book isn't intended as a technical resource, building professionals may want to use it as a launching point for discussions with clients about approaches to building green.

SEVEN PATHS TO
A GOOD GREEN HOME

What makes a good home green? What makes a green home good? There's no single definition of green-built housing. Instead, many people refer to *shades of green,* recognizing that there are different paths to building better homes. An energy-efficient home in Louisiana will differ from one in Idaho because they're responding to a very different set of conditions, from climate to culture. A farmhouse can be as green as a townhouse, but they'll express that greenness in unique ways. Still, the concept of green building isn't so broad as to defy description. Principles and practices have evolved—some over hundreds of years and some quite recently—that form the heart of a good green home.

This book lays out seven fundamental principles of green building, illustrated by photographs of homes that exemplify various shades of green—each one shows a different step along the path to creating a better home. While most of the homes shown here are located in the western United States and Canada, they represent various types of homes, from traditional to modern, urban to rural, modest to luxurious. Although there may be differences between what works in these homes and what may be appropriate in yours, many of the approaches featured here can be tailored to your circumstances.

The first chapter, *Know Where You Are,* recognizes that where you live affects both the quality of your life *and* the quality of the environment. Whether you're redecorating, remodeling, buying a new house, or building from scratch, understanding the unique characteristics of your particular place can help you create a greener home. The second chapter, *Size Matters,* takes on the subject of why bigger isn't always better (at least, when it comes to homes). *You Have the Power* discusses ways you can take charge of the energy you use. *Build for Today and Tomorrow* recognizes that a well-built home will have long-term benefits for you and for future generations. *Clean Living: Protecting Our Air and Water* covers what you can do at home to protect two of our most precious resources. *Build a Better Wall* presents alternatives to conventional construction methods. Finally, *Use the Right Stuff* encourages wise use of materials to keep your home healthy and our planet thriving.

If seven principles sound like a lot to tackle, don't lose heart. Greening your home is a process. The goal is not creating a perfect home, but creating a better home. Small steps and the right attitude can lead to big changes. Learn a little, do a little, laugh a lot, don't beat yourself up over what you can't get done, and take the time to plant some flowers along the path to a good green home.

Left: Good green homes come in every color—not just green! Green building means creating beautiful homes that meet our needs and aspirations, while ensuring we leave our world healthy enough so that future generations can meet theirs.

know WHERE you are

When it comes to sustainability, where do you begin? Is it possible—or desirable— to have a good green home without addressing the sustainability of your neighborhood or wider community? It's a chicken-and-egg dilemma. Do you paint your living room with a nontoxic paint that doesn't pollute the air inside your home, even though there's an outdated power plant in your neighborhood that's polluting the air *outside* your home? Or do you first lobby to get the power plant cleaned up before worrying about the paint on your walls? Do either, both, or find a third, fourth, or fifth solution. The key to change is action. Take a small step. Do something that feels manageable today or this weekend. Then do another thing.

[Do something that feels manageable today or this weekend.]

One place to start is to pay more attention to your surroundings. The closer you look, the better you'll come to understand how the natural environment—as well as the built environment around us—interacts with your home and affects your life. Paying closer attention needn't feel daunting. If your house overheats in the summer, for example, notice the changing path of sunlight through the day and through the seasons. Perhaps you can plant deciduous trees near the west and south walls to provide cooling shade. Come fall, the trees will drop their leaves and the sun's rays will help heat your home during the colder months.

Opposite: Green building is local. What makes sense in one part of the country may not be appropriate elsewhere. Thick rammed-earth walls and small deep-set windows help keep this home cool in Tucson's blistering heat.

Left: This classic farmhouse looks like it's always been here, but it was built recently for a family that runs a dairy farm. Basic green-building principles are at the heart of this home: Don't build bigger than necessary, orient the rooms and windows for good daylighting, and make it energy efficient. A family of six lives in this four-bedroom, three-bath, 2,330-square-foot house. Stealing the scene is Valentine, the children's 4-H cow, who joined the dairy farm around Valentine's Day.

If you're apartment hunting, notice how much daylight each room gets. If you work from home, perhaps you can find an apartment with good northern exposure so that your workspace is illuminated with even, indirect daylight throughout the day.

Notice the direction of the prevailing winds. If you live in a warm climate, breezes may be welcome, but if you live in a place with biting winter gales, you may want to use trees, shrubs, or a fence to deflect them away from your home.

Does paying attention to local conditions mean that a resident of Maine shouldn't live in a Mediterranean-style house? Or that Floridians should disconnect their air conditioners and let their homes become moldy, sweltering saunas? No. A good green home isn't about a particular look. It doesn't require sacrificing comfort or health. On a personal level, it's about combining

the aesthetic that appeals to you with smart building concepts. The Maine home can have the style its owners love without costing a fortune to heat on a wintry night if it's tightly built and well insulated. The Florida home can be sheltered from the sun and cooled with breezes, using air conditioning to supplement, not supplant local conditions.

There's no such thing as a generic good green home. Whether you're remodeling or building a new home, get the most for your money by focusing on the building issues that matter most in your particular location. Strategies that make sense in one place may not in another. Xeriscaping—landscaping to minimize water use—will be more important in arid Phoenix than

Top: At Dewees Island, a private island near Charleston, South Carolina, the developer and property owners have taken extraordinary measures to protect the barrier island's ecologically sensitive habitat. No more than 150 homes will be built on the island's 1,200 acres, with some 65 percent of the land permanently off-limits to development. Photo courtesy Dewees Island.

Opposite: Except for a few service vehicles, Dewees Island is car-free. Residents travel the sand roads by foot, bicycle, or electric golf cart. Photo courtesy Dewees Island.

Above: Where you choose to live has environmental consequences. The homes on this ridge near San Diego are being built on former agricultural land. The builder is mitigating the subdivision's environmental impacts by restoring 150 acres of ecologically sensitive habitat, establishing a wildlife corridor so that animals can move among natural areas, and permanently preserving nearly 750 acres of open space.

rainy Seattle. A white roof that reflects heat will do a lot more good in Honolulu than in Montreal.

On a broader level, creating good green homes is about developing new kinds of communities and enriching existing ones so that everyone is well housed, and that long commutes, high energy bills, and unhealthy building materials become relics of the past. Ultimately, we need healthier and more sustainable neighborhoods, communities, and natural areas as much as we need our own personal spaces to be greener and healthier. This book focuses on steps some people have taken—and things you might want to do—to create more sustainable personal places. But there's a larger world out there that needs tending, so as you envision what your own home could be, also imagine what's possible beyond your own good green walls.

> A good green home isn't about a particular look.

LIVE CLOSE TO YOUR LIFE

We've heard about the downsides of suburban sprawl—those brand-new subdivisions, strip malls, and office parks that keep extending the boundaries of development. Sprawl eats up agricultural and recreational land. It impinges on ecologically important habitats. It's inextricably linked to traffic congestion and pollution woes associated with an automobile-based lifestyle.

There are alternatives to sprawl and to spending hours of every day in a car. Consider living in a city, for example, or in an older suburb where the houses are built within walking distance of a village center. Take a look at the New Urbanist or transit-oriented developments that are cropping up in some regions. Seek out communities that promote smart growth management, communities that try to balance housing needs with open space and agricultural land protection.

When choosing a home, consider its location in relation to other places you need to get to: work, schools, stores, movie theaters, doctors, parks. Are there mass transit lines? How far will you have to drive? Look for neighborhoods with safe walking, bicycling, and public transit options that connect to where you need to go. Some seemingly innocuous details, such as the way a neighborhood's streets are laid out, can have a major effect on the quality of your life. In gated communities or neighborhoods where cul-de-sacs predominate, you usually need a car to get to a store or even to visit a friend who lives on the other side of the development. But in communities where the streets are laid out in an old-fashioned grid pattern, the

Above: This mixed-use infill development in southeast Portland, Oregon, combines high density and good living. Built on the site of a former commercial dairy operation, the Belmont Dairy complex includes 26,000 square feet of retail space and eighty-five apartments. Right: An adjacent development features thirty row houses clustered around landscaped pedestrian courtyards.

Above and right: This new development embraces many of the principles of New Urbanism, with houses clustered closer than in more conventional subdivisions. Private yards are small but there's plenty of community green space, and walking and biking trails. New Urbanist communities are often designed to de-emphasize the role of cars in our lives, with garages set back from the street or accessed from a rear alley. The neighborhoods tend to be built to a human scale, with narrow streets that calm traffic and encourage walking. Many such developments provide a diversity of housing types, with detached houses, town homes, and even apartment buildings sharing the same block. The development shown here, near Portland, Oregon, includes a mixed-use district modeled after an old-fashioned Main Street, with apartments built over ground-floor commercial space and a new city hall anchoring the block.

Right: This mixed-use building in Portland, Oregon, built by an innovative partnership between the public library system and a private developer, combines a library, affordable and market-rate apartments, and a café. This high-density housing provides an alternative to suburban sprawl by taking advantage of the "air space" above the library.

streets are connected—making it easier for you to walk and bicycle from here to there.

If you're attracted to a distant suburb because the housing there seems cheaper, factor in the cost to your household of owning multiple cars, as well as the energy and time you'll spend commuting and chauffeuring your children. Consider living in a mixed-use neighborhood where homes, stores, offices, and other businesses share the same area instead of being segregated into separate zones connected only by automobiles. Work from home if you can or live as close to work as possible—you'll save money, reduce pollution, and give yourself the priceless gift of time.

No matter where you choose to live, there are steps you can take to make your home more sustainable. The next three sections offer suggestions on how to green an existing home, what to look for when buying a new home, and ideas to consider if you're planning to build your own home.

LIVING IN A "PRE-OWNED" HOME

While many of us dream of building a home or of buying a brand-new home, the reality is that most of us live in homes that have changed hands a few—or even a few dozen—times. In the United States today, there are more than 107 million existing housing units. Improving their environmental performance may be even more of a challenge than the greening of new homes. Older homes are often less energy efficient—and less comfortable—than new homes. They may have moisture-related problems, such as mold, condensation, or rot. Some are burdened by materials and products that we once thought harmless, such as asbestos insulation, lead-based paints, or underground oil tanks.

Opposite: This bungalow underwent a thoroughly green remodel, including the use of certified sustainably harvested wood for the framing, floors, and exterior siding.

Right: In this child's bedroom, part of an addition to a home listed on the National Register of Historic Places, new energy-efficient double-pane windows increase comfort and save energy. All the new framing lumber and hardwood flooring was FSC-certified to have come from sustainably managed forests.

There's much that can be done to transform a good older home into a good green home. Green remodeling, however, does have more inherent constraints than building from scratch. It may be impossible, for instance, to change an existing building's orientation to take better advantage of daylight and the sun's heat. It may be too costly to replace old single-pane windows with double-pane, energy-efficient windows. Still, from a resource-consumption standpoint, a pre-owned home usually represents a better choice than a new home, since no new trees were felled for lumber, no new site was cleared of vegetation, and no new roads or other infrastructure were built to service the home.

GOOD GREEN REMODELING

The principles of green remodeling are basically the same as the principles of building a new green home. Your remodeling project can be an opportunity to improve your home's energy efficiency. You can also take a fresh look at how you use your home and what's the right-sized space for how you live. The old adage "bigger is better" doesn't necessarily apply when it comes to homes. If you're contemplating an addition, ask yourself whether you really do need more room. If your place feels cramped because it's overwhelmed with clutter, adding more square footage may not make a difference in the long run, since stuff seems to accumulate in direct proportion to the amount of space that's available.

Sometimes problems such as gloomy rooms and awkward layouts can be solved through interior design changes instead of expensive, stressful, and resource-consuming remodeling. White or light-colored paint on ceilings and walls will make rooms remarkably brighter by reflecting daylight deeper into the space. Replacing heavy draperies with sheer curtains is another way to bring in more light and make a space feel larger.

[Take a fresh look at how you use your home and what's the right-sized space for how you live.]

Also look at whether changing the function of some rooms might solve your space crunch. Can a rarely used guest room double as a home office? Perhaps that formal dining room that's used only a few times a year can do double duty as a study or a place for working on hobbies and projects. Don't feel restricted by how a room originally was intended to be used. It's your home—make it work for you!

GOOD GREEN RECOMMENDATIONS:
GREEN REMODELING

■ *Ask for what you want.* When you're interviewing architects, designers, or contractors for your remodeling project, discuss your green building interests at the start. Don't wait until after you've signed a contract to surprise them with your green wish list. Energy efficiency and smart resource use need to be integrated into the entire remodeling process, not tacked on at the end. If you rent a home that's due for a new coat of paint, a new carpet, or more extensive upgrades, talk with your landlord about your green home interests. If you raise the subject in a constructive way, you may be pleasantly surprised by your landlord's willingness to consider new ideas.

■ *Put energy efficiency at the top of your list.* Consider improving the insulation in ceilings, floors, and walls. Make sure that heating and cooling ducts are connected and well sealed at their joints. Weather strip and caulk around windows and doors to reduce drafts. If it's time to replace old appliances or heating and cooling equipment, select more energy-efficient models. If your remodeling plans call for new windows, specify high-performance glazing.

■ *Design for how you live.* Don't add a lot of formal space if you lead a casual lifestyle. Many people are finding that formal living or dining rooms and grand foyers don't fit the way they live today. It's your home—live in it the way that suits you.

■ *Redecorate rather than replace.* Each year, millions of homeowners rip out their kitchens or bathrooms. Most of what is removed winds up in landfills. But there are alternatives to full-scale remodeling. Cabinets can be refaced to give them a fresh look. Faucets can be updated without replacing the entire sink, and sinks and tubs can be re-coated to look brand-new.

■ *Use safe and resource-smart building materials.* Use water-based finishes and interior paints with low- or zero-volatile organic compounds (VOCs). These emit fewer air pollutants than conventional alternatives. Use materials and products that are durable and easy to maintain so that you don't have to replace them frequently or spend time and money keeping them in good shape. Look for materials with recycled content. Consider using locally manufactured products when possible—the fewer miles a product travels, the more fuel is saved.

■ *Deconstruct rather than demolish* the portions of the house you're going to remodel. There's almost no end to the materials that can be salvaged, including moldings, cabinets, appliances, light fixtures, and bricks. Reuse, sell, or donate the old stuff. Check with your local government's waste management agency or recycling office for tips on what to do with used building materials in your area.

■ *Don't use wood from old-growth trees.* Our ancient forests are irreplaceable, and they're rapidly disappearing. You can't necessarily tell from looking at a piece of lumber whether it's from an old-growth tree. One handy rule-of-thumb for large-dimension lumber is that if it's free of knots and larger than 2 x 8 inches, it's most likely from an old-growth tree. A better alternative is to look for reclaimed lumber or wood that's been certified by the Forest Stewardship Council (FSC) or a similarly reputable organization to have come from a sustainably managed forest.

Above: The owners increased the development density of this property by raising the two-story house and adding ground-floor office space. They thoroughly renovated the two flats on the second and third floors. Insulation made from recycled newspaper fills the wall and ceiling cavities, creating quieter, more comfortable and energy-efficient homes. Windows and skylights were added to improve daylighting and passive solar heating.

Right: Small rooms were opened up to create more usable space and let in light. A contemporary open plan provides zones rather than separate rooms for living, dining, and cooking.

RESOURCEFUL RENOVATION

An old home's limitations can sometimes be turned to an advantage. When Cate Leger and Karl Wanaselja bought this two-unit Victorian-era house in Berkeley, California, they found themselves with a handsome old building that had been long neglected but showed promise. The property, which includes an adjacent small building that had housed an antiques shop, is well situated for urban living and working. It's close to shops, neighborhood services, and public transit lines, and is surrounded by a mix of houses and apartment buildings.

One drawback to the house is that it fronts a heavily trafficked street, with a small setback. Cate and Karl, both architects specializing in ecologically intelligent design, made the most of this. Since they needed to replace the original brick foundation anyway, they jacked up the building and added a whole floor of office space at street level. This created a buffer between the residential units and the street, providing the flats with more privacy and tranquility. The office space, which the couple sold after completing the renovations, has large windows that look out on the busy street, creating a more interesting view for passersby than a blank wall or a garage door. Finding ways to use urban properties more intensively by adding residential or commercial units to an existing building, as Cate and Karl did here, or by building on underused or vacant city lots, is an important strategy in helping to revitalize urban areas and reduce suburban sprawl.

Above the ground floor, the couple opened up the cramped rooms by judiciously removing walls and adding windows and skylights to create two bright and spacious flats. They sold the lower flat and now live, along with their young daughter, in the sun-drenched, 1,000-square-foot top flat. They run their architectural practice out of the remodeled building next door.

Top: This richly grained counter was milled from a bay laurel tree felled by a storm. The kitchen-sink counter (above) sparkles with polished chips of recycled glass.

A new bathroom tucks into the roof's slope. Part of the roof was replaced with a skylight that has a special mirrored film between panes of glass to help block some of the sun's heat. The center panel opens for ventilation, while translucent lower panels provide privacy. A shaving mirror (inset) mounted next to the sink led a previous life as a car's side-view mirror.

Top left: During the renovation, the original interior was carefully dismantled. The owners reused flooring, doors, molding, and many other materials, and sold surplus trim to a building supply company. Buildings contribute to our collective memory—they tell us stories about where we come from and who we are. Adapting buildings to today's needs while retaining connections to our past is an important facet of green building.

Top right: Railings made from Volvo hatchback doors prompt a smile when visitors come up the stairs.

Left: The top flat's deck includes salvaged elements used in ways that are both whimsical and functional, such as pickup truck tailgates that serve as railings and benches.

A particularly engaging aspect of this home is the whimsical way in which Cate and Karl incorporated all kinds of salvaged materials. Curved glass awnings above exterior doors were once automobile hatchbacks. Pickup truck tailgates have been fashioned into deck railings and benches. In a bathroom, a car's side-view mirror is mounted on a wall as a shaving mirror. These touches are playful and thought provoking—and they gently reassure us that it's possible to have a sense of humor, a sense of style, and still be green.

BUYING A NEW HOME:
HOW GREEN ARE YOUR CHOICES?

When it comes to purchasing a brand-new home from a developer, buyers generally have little or no influence over the features, systems, and equipment that determine how healthy and sustainable the home will be. Except in the case of custom-designed houses, which are discussed in the following section, builders usually predetermine everything from the direction the windows face to the efficiency of the heating and cooling systems that are installed. Buyers could use their purchasing clout to insist that homes be built to a high environmental standard. Instead, most buyers are limited to cosmetic decisions: Solid-surface or granite counters? Four-burner or five-burner range? White or almond bathtub?

What's a homebuyer to do? Ultimately, it's up to consumers to demand that every home

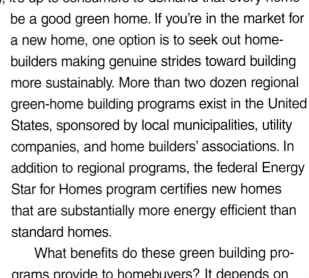

be a good green home. If you're in the market for a new home, one option is to seek out homebuilders making genuine strides toward building more sustainably. More than two dozen regional green-home building programs exist in the United States, sponsored by local municipalities, utility companies, and home builders' associations. In addition to regional programs, the federal Energy Star for Homes program certifies new homes that are substantially more energy efficient than standard homes.

What benefits do these green building programs provide to homebuyers? It depends on the program, but a built-green certification often means that the home exceeds local energy code requirements, which keeps your home more comfortable and saves you money year after year. Improvements may include better insulation, high-performance windows, efficient heating and air conditioning equipment, and tighter construction that reduces drafts, air leakage, and moisture infiltration.

Above and opposite: Pardee Homes has committed to meeting the U.S. Energy Star standard for all its new houses. Their Living Smart program (introduced in a San Diego, California, subdivision) offers an array of green features. Standard items include spectrally selective low-e windows for energy efficiency and comfort, carpet made from recycled plastic bottles, and driveway pavers designed to reduce storm water runoff. Buyers can customize their homes with various green options, including a photovoltaic system to generate electricity from sunlight, a tankless water heater, Energy Star–labeled kitchen appliances, and low-VOC paint.

The home shown on the previous two pages is in a subdivision that sits on former agricultural land, above a canyon of unique habitat called southern maritime chaparral. As part of its development agreement, Pardee undertook a 150-acre restoration project to preserve habitat for many species of wildlife native to the region. Workers removed invasive nonnative plants from the canyon, replacing them with native plants raised from seed in a temporary nursery.

Other benefits may include plumbing fixtures that reduce water use, and healthier materials that don't introduce harmful pollutants into your home.

These programs often require participating builders to undergo some training in the principles and practices of green building. Standards vary from basic self-certification checklists to rigorous compliance requirements verified by an independent third party. Some builders have developed their own green building standards that they apply to all or some of the new homes they build.

Beware, though, of companies engaged in "greenwashing"—the practice of making deceptive claims about environmental performance. Some builders have been known to co-opt the language of sustainability without substantively changing their practices.

GOOD **GREEN** RECOMMENDATIONS: FINDING A **GREEN-BUILT** HOME

■ *Support green builders.* If you're in the market for a brand-new home, look for homebuilders with green building experience. The U.S. Environmental Protection Agency's Energy Star Website lists homebuilders who build Energy Star–labeled homes. State and local environmental agencies often have a staff person who is knowledgeable about green building issues and who can point you in the right direction. Also try contacting your local Home Builders Association (HBA), an association of homebuilders and remodelers with chapters throughout the United States. Some regional HBAs sponsor programs that certify green builders.

■ *Ask for good green homes.* Healthy, environmentally responsible homes will become the norm only if we start demanding them. Whenever you're in a builder's sales office, ask about their approach to green building. Here are some questions to ask:

Did the builder take any steps to improve the home's energy efficiency beyond minimum levels required by building code?

How was indoor air quality taken into account when materials, equipment, and finishes were chosen?

What was on the building site previously? Was it undeveloped land? If so, did the builder do anything to compensate for the loss of open space?

During construction, were steps taken to protect the natural environment of the site (beyond what is required by local building codes)? Was vegetation preserved? Were ecologically sensitive areas protected?

If the new homes are part of a large development, is the neighborhood designed to make it convenient for people to walk, bicycle, or take public transit to work, school, stores, and other places they need to get to? Are there public parks and open space? Are the homes designed to foster a sense of community and neighborliness (e.g., front porches, garages set back from the street)?

■ *Improve on the standard plan.* If the new home you're buying is still under construction, look for opportunities to improve how it's being built and finished. Ask the sales and design-center staff about ways to make your home more energy efficient, healthy, and comfortable. For example, you may be able to request appliances and heating and cooling equipment that are substantially more efficient than standard models. You may be able to select interior paints that don't pollute the air, or flooring made from beautiful bamboo or sustainably harvested wood. Smaller building companies may have more flexibility to address individual needs than large builders. Major changes may not be possible, but you won't know unless you ask.

home profile

THREE HOMES IN THE CITY

In an area of northeast Portland dubbed the Alberta Arts District, thanks to its vibrant gallery scene, three new homes are clustered on what was once the large side yard of a 1929 Dutch Colonial house. The new homes are a prime example of urban infill: building on—or "filling in"—vacant or underused lots within a city. Urban infill makes good green sense. It takes advantage of existing urban infrastructure such as roads, utilities, and public transit. It reduces sprawl and can help revitalize our cities' older neighborhoods.

> **Urban infill makes good green sense.**

After remodeling and selling the Dutch Colonial, David Hassin of Terrafirma Building partitioned its side yard, and then sited and built the infill complex to harmonize with the surrounding residences. The three new homes are small compared to the average American house being built today, but with their Craftsman-style detailing, ample daylighting, and contemporary floor plans, they feel solid and spacious.

The larger of the houses, at about 1,600 square feet, has a city-sized front garden and a small backyard, with a detached garage accessed via a rear alley. The other two homes are 1,400-square-foot row houses, each with two bedrooms, a small backyard, and a one-car garage. A shared wall between the row houses helps make them more energy efficient than a typical detached house. These city homes are situated along a public transit line, with restaurants, markets, and other neighborhood amenities within walking distance.

David made a point of using healthy, environmentally sustainable materials throughout. Inside, paints and finishes with no- or low-VOCs were used (VOCs are a class of potentially harmful chemicals that readily emit fumes at room temperature). The maple flooring was FSC-certified to have come from well-managed forests, while the carpets are made of recycled plastic bottles. To keep the homes comfortable, David selected low-e windows with an argon-gas fill and a U-factor lower than required by local building codes

Above: These three homes were certified to meet the standards of the local utility's green building program. The program included tests of the air-tightness of the homes, and inspections to ensure that energy and air-quality equipment and materials were properly installed.

Left: Craftsman-style detailing and environmentally friendly features make for gracious living in this 1,600-square-foot, three-bedroom home.

Below left: True linoleum covers the kitchen and bathroom floors. It's made primarily from renewable raw materials, including sawdust, linseed oil, pine rosin, natural pigments, and jute.

(see page 56 for more about energy-efficient window characteristics). David built the homes on spec (all three sold while still under construction), so he kept a careful eye on budget. Some of the materials and equipment he selected cost more than conventional products. The high-efficiency furnaces, for example, cost more upfront but will save money for the homeowners year after year. He also installed fresh-air ventilation systems that introduce outside air into the homes at regular intervals and draw out stale inside air. Although they were an added expense, David decided to include them to help ensure that the homes would be comfortable and healthy throughout the year. The low-VOC paint cost a little more than standard paint, but it, too, contributes to a healthier indoor environment. And it's hard to put a price on that.

On Dewees Island, near Charleston, South Carolina, the island's architectural resources board scrutinizes every proposed home design to ensure that it meets the island's environmental and architectural standards. Healthy materials, careful site planning, the use of native vegetation, and water conservation are emphasized. A home's construction may not permanently disturb more than 7,500 square feet of land, and trees and understory growth can't be removed without approval. Photo © Rick Rhodes.

Rather than perching this Northern Californian home on a knoll, the owners and their architects decided to nestle it in a saddle between hills, where it is sheltered and doesn't overshadow the landscape.

BUILDING A CUSTOM GOOD GREEN HOME

Building an environmentally friendly home can be an exciting, rewarding experience. It's an opportunity to create a dwelling that's respectful of the land and community you're a part of. It's a chance to put your heart and values into a structure that may last long after you've moved on.

Building green isn't without its frustrations, of course—from dealing with tradespeople who may not share your goals to tracking down products that may be in short supply. Sometimes compromises have to be made. You may decide to choose a different type of hardwood flooring after you learn that the one you had your heart set on comes from an unsustainably harvested forest. Or you may wind up forgoing the electricity-generating photovoltaic system you dreamed of because it blows your budget.

> Building any home from the ground up always involves compromises and challenges.

But building *any* home from the ground up always involves compromises and challenges. If you do decide to go green, be prepared for some additional bumps in the road. Keep in mind that the goal isn't building a perfect home, but building a better home.

GOOD GREEN RECOMMENDATIONS:
BUILDING A CUSTOM HOME

■ *Assemble a good green team* that's as excited about collaborating on your home as you are, and that's experienced in green design and building practices. You don't need to be a green building expert yourself—that's your team's job. But first you'll want to make sure that they're up for the challenge. When you interview designers and builders, in addition to the usual questions, ask about their green building experience.

■ *Consider the location's ecological sensitivity.* Avoid building on land that will be slow to recover from site disturbances. Examples of ecologically sensitive areas include floodplains, wetlands, extremely steep slopes prone to erosion, and land that's known to be a habitat for threatened or endangered species. From an ecological perspective, building on previously developed land is often preferable to building on a "greenfield"—prime agricultural land or open space that has never been developed.

■ *Get oriented.* Too often, homes seem oriented primarily to impress others (with their longest side facing the street, for example, so as to look more imposing). Try to position the home, its rooms, and windows in relation to the land and the sun and for the benefit of the people who will live in it. To create a home that's naturally illuminated by daylight and warmed in the winter by the sun, it's usually best to site the building with its longer wall (or most of its windows) facing south. If you're building in a high-density urban neighborhood, this may be more difficult to achieve—but building in an urban area has many other environmental advantages that compensate for orientation constraints.

■ *Know your land.* Take some time to get to know your property's unique features. Whether you're building on an urban, suburban, or rural lot, try to spend time there at different hours of the day and night and during different seasons, if possible. Watch and listen. Discover where the prevailing winds come from and what plants and animals make themselves at home on your land. Study the path the sun takes over your property. Talk with locals about the area's weather patterns. Be aware of the consequences of where you site your home. Will the topography shelter or expose your building? Will neighboring buildings provide welcoming shade or block needed daylight? Consider how noise, wind, and the flow of storm water will affect and be affected by your building. Make sure your design and building team is knowledgeable about the interactions between the built and the natural environment.

■ *Study older homes.* Look at homes built in your area before central heating and air conditioning made it possible to build any style of home anywhere. Older homes often offer important clues for how to design in tune with the local climate. In Charleston, South Carolina, for example, many older homes have generous wraparound porches that shade windows and walls from the punishing summer heat, with shutters that can be closed to ward off sunlight or opened to let in cooling breezes.

■ *Do not disturb.* Before starting to build, work with your team to develop a plan so that your site is disrupted as little as possible. Include this plan in your construction contract. By reducing disruptions, you won't have to replace as much topsoil later. Your utility bills may be lower if you've preserved mature trees that provide summer shade and block winter winds. One step for limiting site disturbance is to make sure that the construction boundaries are clearly marked. Also, designate areas for materials staging, equipment storage, recyclable items, construction waste, and concrete truck washout. Indicate which trees and other vegetation will remain. Remember that the larger the home's footprint, the more natural area you'll wind up displacing.

BRIDGING TOWN AND COUNTRY

Woolen Mills, a historic neighborhood on the edge of downtown Charlottesville, Virginia, has a village feel, with an eclectic mix of homes and abundant natural areas. The neighborhood, which takes its name from a mill built on the Rivanna River before the Civil War, has managed to retain its rural character while still feeling connected to the city. It's here that Allison Ewing and Chris Hays built a home on a half-acre property that slopes to the south, with views of rooftops, of a steepled chapel, and, when the leaves are off the trees, of Monticello, Thomas Jefferson's storied home. Their property is close to schools and shops, and only a mile and half from where the couple work as architects at William McDonough + Partners, an internationally respected sustainable design firm.

When the couple found the property, they didn't have a particular design in mind; in fact, they'd originally been looking for an older home to renovate rather than build from scratch. Once they owned the lot, time and budget constraints meant they couldn't begin building immediately. They spent a year or two becoming acquainted with the land, thinking about what kind of home would work best on the site, and gradually honing their design ideas. Eventually, as their plans coalesced, they teamed up with builder Craig DuBose. Along with his skills as a builder, Craig brought to the project a heartfelt interest in the philosophies and practice of building green.

Together they created a 2,400-square-foot home that sits on the property's northern edge. From the street, the home is entered through a pivoting gate that opens onto a breezeway separating the two portions of the house. The main portion contains open living, dining, and kitchen areas and a powder room downstairs; two

A pivoting front gate opens onto a breezeway reminiscent of a Southern dogtrot-style house. The experience of entering a home only to find oneself still outside creates a subtle sense of drama and expectation, while helping to establish the home's sense of place and its connection to the land. A bridge crosses over the breezeway, connecting the home's two parts. Photo © 2003 Prakash Patel.

children's bedrooms, a play loft, bathroom, and laundry are above. A second-story enclosed bridge crosses over the breezeway to the master bedroom and bath, which sit above a work studio that doubles as a guest room. All the service spaces are clustered on the north side, allowing the living spaces to open up to the south light and views.

This southern exposure proved ideal for passive solar heating—the home is designed so that the low-angle winter sun enters through the south-facing windows and warms the house, reducing the need for mechanical heating. Air conditioning cools and dehumidifies the home during Charlottesville's sweltering summers, but for much of the year open windows provide cooling cross-breezes. Full-height windows shaded by a unique system of exterior louvered panels allow in some direct beams of sunlight, but not so much that it's uncomfortably hot or bright. After four years in the house, Allison and Chris say they still notice the light as it moves through their home, its changing patterns calling quiet attention to the hour and the season and the pleasure of a simple moment.

Opposite: A 600-square-foot deck extends the home's livable space. The deck opens onto a backyard landscaped mainly with indigenous plants. At the property's southern edge, the owners created a wetland area and a pond. Rainwater from the roof is directed to the pond rather than running off the property. Photo © 2003 Prakash Patel.

Left: The home is situated on the property's northern end with the main living spaces facing south. Louvered panels shade the south-facing windows in the summer, while the low-angle sun helps heat the home in the winter. Low-e windows keep the home comfortable and save energy. Photo © 2003 Prakash Patel.

Below: Upstairs, a balcony that serves as a play area opens onto the double-height living room. FSC-certified wood was used for framing the south and interior walls, and for the interior trim, windows, and doors. The exposed heart-pine columns, Douglas fir beams inside, and Douglas fir columns outside were reclaimed from abandoned factories. The north, east, and west walls were built of structural insulated panels (SIPs), which create a tight, energy-efficient building envelope. Photo © 2003 Prakash Patel.

SIZE
matters

Our houses are bulking up. In 1970, the average new U.S. home was about 1,500 square feet. By 2001, it had grown to more than 2,300 square feet, even as the average number of people per household continued to shrink. Even manufactured houses—once known as mobile homes—are joining the bigger-is-better game, with the occasional triple-wide exceeding 3,000 square feet!

Call them what you will—McMansions, trophy houses, monster homes, starter castles, muscle houses—very large homes have become a formidable trend in home building today. They offer specialized single-use spaces that pile on the square footage: en suite bathrooms for every bedroom; master suites with wet bars, refrigerators, and cappuccino machines; butler's pantries; home theaters; exercise rooms; meditation spaces; gift-wrapping rooms.

Where do we draw the line from an environmental perspective? Can a 12,000-square-foot home ever be considered green? How about 5,000 square feet, or 4,000?

[Can a 12,000-square-foot home ever be considered green? ·]

Green building guidelines usually start with the premise that smaller is better. Sounds reasonable, but isn't there something about this principle that rankles just a bit? Could it be that "small" evokes images of cramped office cubicles, closet-sized Manhattan apartments, and airline seats with too little leg room? And who decides how small a home should be? Are we going to legislate the amount of square feet each person is entitled to, or place a luxury tax on homes over a certain size, or require people with unused bedrooms to take in boarders?

Perhaps it won't come to that, thanks to growing awareness of the benefits of homes designed to a more livable size. Compared to very large homes, smaller homes are typically gentler on the environment *and* on the people who live in them. They require fewer materials to

Opposite: Built-in storage uses space efficiently without increasing a home's square footage.

GOOD **GREEN** RECOMMENDATIONS:
RIGHT-SIZED LIVING

■ *Assess your needs.* Most people, regardless of the size of their homes, spend the bulk of their time in just a few rooms—the kitchen, the bedrooms, and the family room. More square footage doesn't necessarily lead to greater satisfaction. Ask yourself how much space you really need. Think of your home as an elegantly tailored suit—you want a perfect fit, neither too loose nor too tight.

■ *Put quality above quantity.* Why spend more money than necessary on rooms that are overly large or that you'll rarely use? Instead, consider putting your money toward high-quality construction that will last, and craftsmanship and materials with true distinction.

■ *Simplify.* Focus on elegant simplicity instead of size, timelessness instead of trendiness. Simplifying often requires a more thoughtful approach to design. It's easy to build big—that's the brute-force method of design. To create a smaller home that works well requires more attention but may ultimately yield a more rewarding home.

■ *Do more with less.* Make rooms serve more than one function. A guestroom that's only used occasionally, for example, can double as a study.

■ *Be flexible.* If you think you might need more space in the future, consider buying a house that's right for today's needs but that could be expanded if you later find you do need more room.

■ *Make the most of the layout.* Look for smaller homes that feel spacious and are effectively laid out—open enough to provide a good flow for entertaining, while still offering spaces that feel intimate. Strategies for making smaller homes live larger include incorporating high ceilings and lofts, forgoing formal rooms that will be infrequently used, shortening or eliminating hallways, and building in seating and storage. Also, a space will feel roomier if there are long lines of sight—either views of the outdoors or views from one room into another. Outdoor spaces—patios, covered or screened porches, and decks—can also effectively extend a home's livable space.

■ *Pare down your stuff.* If you need a bigger home to warehouse all your belongings, consider other solutions, such as built-in shelves, cabinets, and storage systems that make the most of underused space. Take a fresh look at your possessions now and then—it could be time for a garage sale or a trip to Goodwill!

■ *Keep the footprint small.* A sprawling house disturbs more land than a compact house. If you're adding on or building a new house, consider building up instead of out.

■ *Make it green.* If you must have a large house, make it as green as you can. Choose a home designed for passive solar heating and daylighting. Make sure the building envelope is tight and energy efficient. Use wood wisely by considering certified wood, engineered lumber, and wood-efficient framing strategies. Find ways to incorporate recycled or salvaged materials in your home's construction and furnishings.

When thoughtfully designed and built with care, a small home may offer more value and satisfaction per square foot than a McMansion. Building smaller allows builders and homeowners to put more of their budget into quality details and materials.

build, create less waste during construction, and eat up less land. They are easier and less expensive to heat, cool, furnish, clean, and maintain.

Whether you're renting, buying, or building a home, consider how much space you really need. You may be surprised by how little your home's square footage has to do with the things that really make you happy. Is it truly more and bigger rooms you're longing for or do you desire a different kind of home—a home that expresses your values, a home with heart?

THE REMAINDER HOUSE

Don Gurney, an architect and the owner of this home tucked into a wooded slope on Bowen Island near Vancouver, British Columbia, didn't specifically set out to create a green home. And yet, motivated by twin passions for the island's natural beauty and the distinctive qualities of reclaimed wood, that's exactly what he did.

Don's quarter-acre property boasts mature cedars, Douglas firs, West Coast maples, and views of the shimmering Howe Sound. But for the past fifty years or so, since this hillside neighborhood was originally subdivided, that quarter-acre had remained undeveloped. It was an awkward wedge of land wrapped on two sides by a road, with homes directly above and below it on the slope. On the subdivision's plans, it was even labeled "remainder lot," a name that Don has adopted for what he fittingly calls the "Remainder House."

Don, who was a bachelor when he bought the lot, imagined building a home of old reclaimed timber. The appeal was not only the beauty of old wood, but also its durability, strength, and dimensional stability—qualities uncommon in today's new wood. His vision for the home didn't come together until he discovered an old 900-foot-long warehouse on the mainland that was slated to be razed. He purchased two bays and both ends of the warehouse, and had the lumber barged to his island property. Don used this reclaimed Douglas fir for virtually all the wood in the home, with the exception of the framing studs and the floor joists on the main

Above: This home sits lightly on the land. Not a single tree was cut on the small wooded lot. Even the roots of an old-growth Douglas fir (at left) were spared. Instead of digging a belowground foundation that would have disturbed the roots, a ground-level grade beam supports that end of the house.

Opposite: Weathered Douglas fir reclaimed from an abandoned warehouse adds character to this distinctive home. The living room, as seen from the bedroom loft, is wrapped on the south and east sides by glass, letting in dappled sunlight. High clerestory windows allow daylight to penetrate deep into the loft.

An elongated patio serves as the home's entryway. In the summer, friends and family gather for meals at long tables and benches set outside.

> [The house is, as Don says, "enough building for this site."]

floor. The wood was milled on site, with Don's builder making board-by-board decisions about how to put each piece of wood to best use.

With just over 610 square feet on its main level and 300 square feet in the loft, the house is, as Don says, "enough building for this site." From the back the house is low-slung, with a curved copper roof that just peeks over the narrow road. The living spaces—indoors and out—face south to take advantage of views of the water and to capture sunlight filtering through the towering trees. In fact, the south side of the house is predominantly transparent, with large windows, glass corner walls, and clerestories, as well as glass doors that open onto patios and terraced areas. This transparency, along with the open-plan interior, makes the house live larger than one might expect. Although it was originally designed by and for a bachelor, it has adapted well to the changes that life brings, and now shelters Don, his wife Saffron, and their two young children.

Above: Designed to harmonize with the landscape and respect neighbors' views and light, the curved copper roof barely rises above street level.

A COTTAGE FOR ONE OR TWO

Nestled on the shore of a sparkling pond, this cluster of ten cottages has the nostalgic feel of a vacation get-away. But it's actually a new residential neighborhood in a rapidly developing suburb fifteen minutes from down-town Portland, Oregon. The pond forms part of a nearly 100-acre city park—with twenty-five acres donated to the city by the cottages' developer, Michael McKeel. Architect Ross Chapin, whose firm specializes in delight-fully scaled homes clustered into "pocket neighbor-hoods," designed the cottages. This compact develop-ment was thoughtfully planned to have minimal impact on the land. It's also intended to help foster a sense of community—the homes are clustered so that they draw residents together, while providing each household with the privacy that comes with having a home of one's own.

Even though each house sits on a lot that's less than 2,000 square feet—with all ten homes taking up less than a half-acre—the homes don't feel hemmed in. A walkway provides a subtle boundary between the cottages and the more public areas, including a "village green" that serves as a common front yard and a community build-ing alongside the shore. A tiny lawn and planting beds in front of each house further define the private zone, while covered front porches provide a transition between the outdoors and the private domain inside. Deep over-hangs above each porch offer shelter from sun and rain.

While the average new home in the United States is now larger than 2,300 square feet, the cottages in this neighborhood are considerably smaller—the four floor plans range from about 950 square feet to 1,300 square feet. While their size may be scaled down, their abundant charm, efficient layouts,

Above: Clustered at the edge of a pond that was once a gravel quarry, this pocket neighborhood of downsized homes is big on amenities, including delightful front porches, a community building at water's edge, a village green fronting the homes, and views of snowcapped Mount Hood.

Left: Raised ceilings, a skylight above the dining area, and built-in storage lend a sense of spaciousness to this 1,300-square-foot cottage.

Opposite top: A community building with a covered porch provides a place for meetings, parties, and taking it easy.

Opposite bottom: Unlike most new suburban developments, where residents drive into garages and disappear inside their houses, here cars are parked in detached garages behind the homes. Residents enter their homes via a pleasant walkway that passes in front of the cottages.

In the bedroom, a lower ceiling creates an intimate atmosphere. Light-colored surfaces reflect daylight to keep the room bright, while windows on two walls encourage cross-breezes. The wood floor is reclaimed Southern heart pine.

and quality workmanship are proof that good things come in small packages. With one and two bedrooms as well as generous loft spaces, these homes are well suited to singles, couples with no children, empty nesters, and even parents with one child.

Inside the cottages, windows are carefully positioned to let in abundant daylight and cooling cross-breezes while providing privacy from neighboring homes. Upstairs, skylights in the lofts open to allow hot air to flow out, helping the homes stay comfortable in the summer without air conditioning. Plenty of storage, including walk-in closets, standing-height attics, and storage rooms adjacent to the garages, help keep clutter to a minimum. Built-in shelves, kitchen peninsulas, and nooks add to the efficiency of the layout.

But these cottages don't just work because they use resources, energy, and space efficiently. They work because they offer old-world charm combined with modern-world conveniences. They work because they're richly detailed inside and out with craftsmanship and style that's designed to delight and honor the people who live in them. And they work because they create a setting that balances the desire for one's own space with the need for connection with others.

The cottages are naturally cooled with windows positioned to induce cross-ventilation, skylights that open to vent heat, and covered porches to provide shading. The porches are built with cedar reclaimed from an abandoned fish cannery.

At 966 square feet, this is the smallest of the four floor plans. The main floor includes a kitchen, built-in dining nook, living area, bedroom, and bathroom. A space-saving ship's ladder with alternating steps leads to one of this cottage's two lofts. Built-in shelves and cabinets and a raised ceiling help the cottage live larger.

you HAVE the power

Most days, we go about our lives without thinking much about the energy we use. But our demand for energy has adverse consequences, whether we're burning heating oil, natural gas, or wood in our homes, or using electricity that comes from fuel-burning power plants.

Through these direct and indirect means, a typical American home contributes twice as many greenhouse gases to the atmosphere each year as a typical car does. Greenhouse gases, which are primarily the result of burning fossil fuels (including coal, oil, and natural gas), trap heat in our atmosphere, leading to global warming. Global warming is only one of many concerns; respiratory diseases, cancer, mercury poisoning in lakes, and acid rain have all been linked to pollutants emitted by many electric power plants, especially older plants fueled by coal.

We don't even benefit from much of the energy we use in our homes because it's wasted by inefficient appliances, leaky ducts and windows, and poorly insulated walls and roofs. But there is a solution: It's energy efficiency, which simply means wringing more value out of each unit of energy you consume. Energy efficiency doesn't require sacrifice and it can be a great investment: it can make you more comfortable, save you money, and increase the value of your home.

The first two sections of this chapter cover the primary ways in which we use energy in our homes: for lighting, and for powering the equipment and appliances that provide us with convenience and comfort. The final section discusses solar power. Why solar? Because while energy efficiency is at the heart of green building today, the future belongs to producing clean and renewable energy and creating homes that give back to the utility grid more electricity than they consume.

Left: This house, located in a climate where summer days can be hot but aren't overly humid, is kept cool without air conditioning. Roof overhangs shade the clerestory windows, while a trellis allows dappled sunlight onto the deck. Jasmine vines provide cooling shade and a sweet fragrance.

LIGHT UP YOUR LIFE

Illuminating a good green home involves more than merely selecting light fixtures that complement your décor. The key to a beautifully illuminated home that's also comfortable and energy efficient is good window selection and the judicious use of daylight, supplemented by highly efficient electric lighting.

WINDOWS OF OPPORTUNITY

Windows—where would we be without them? They let in daylight, give us a breath of fresh air, protect us from wind, rain, and snow, and connect us to the world outside. But not all windows are created equal. Leaky, uninsulated, unshaded, or improperly oriented windows can make your home too hot, too cold, or uncomfortably drafty.

Today's high-performance windows, which can be twice as energy efficient as windows sold ten years ago, normally have two panes of glass separated by an insulating air gap that blocks some of the heat transfer between indoors and outdoors. This double glazing also blocks sound, making for a quieter home. Sometimes the air gap is filled with a gas, such as argon or krypton, that's an even better insulator than air.

> Today's high-performance windows can be twice as energy efficient as windows sold ten years ago.

It's common these days for an energy-efficient window to have a thin, transparent, low-emissivity (low-e) coating. Standard low-e coatings reflect internal heat back into the room, making the room feel much more comfortable when it's cold outside. In addition to keeping heat in when it's cold outside, "spectrally selective" low-e coatings also block much of the sun's heat from entering through the windows. (This feature is desirable if you live in a hot climate, but is less of an advantage in cold locations where you want to let the sun's warmth into your home.)

Low-e and spectrally selective low-e windows can be a very good value in new homes. In cold climates, low-e windows can cut heating costs by more than 30 percent compared to single-

Double-pane, low-e windows with fiberglass frames help make this farmhouse near Seattle comfortable and energy efficient. Fiberglass window frames may cost more, but they're durable, weather resistant, and won't rot, important considerations in places like the rainy Pacific Northwest.

pane windows. In hot climates, spectrally selective low-e windows can reduce cooling costs by nearly 40 percent. Low-e windows also help reduce fading of fabrics and wood.

In older homes, replacing old single-pane windows with high-performance windows won't necessarily be cost effective based on energy savings alone. Even if the energy savings isn't substantial, however, some homeowners spend the extra money to replace their old windows in order to make their homes more comfortable. If you live in a cold climate, an alternative to replacing single-pane windows is to install storm windows in the winter and to use weather stripping and caulking to reduce drafts and to plug leaks. Insulating shades or curtains can keep the heat in on cold nights.

Good low-tech ways to keep the hot summer sun off your windows include generous eaves, exterior shutters, awnings, and verandas. You can also block some heat gain by using curtains, blinds, and interior shutters, but if you live in a hot climate, it's better to block that harsh sun before it even reaches the outside of your window. Another good green shading strategy is to plant deciduous trees, or deciduous vines on trellises, to shade your home in the summer. In the winter, they'll drop their leaves, allowing more heat and light inside your house.

Most new windows and some skylights in the United States have a National Fenestration Rating Council (NFRC) label to help you compare the energy efficiency of competing products. Some energy-efficient windows also carry an Energy Star label. When you're looking at a window's energy label, it helps to understand these terms:

Solar heat gain coefficient (SHGC) indicates how much of the sun's heat will enter through a window. An SHGC of 0.40, for example, means that 40 percent of the sun's heat gets through the window.

U-factor tells you the window's resistance to heat flow, or the amount of heat a window will lose. Windows with a lower U-factor do a better job of insulating your home.

Visible transmittance indicates how much visible light the glass transmits. Where views and daylighting are important, select windows with high visible transmittance.

Residential window frames are typically wood, vinyl, aluminum, steel, or fiberglass. While there are environmental, financial, and aesthetic arguments for each option, keep in mind that the window's overall energy performance—as shown on the NFRC label—will likely have the biggest long-term impact on your comfort and your wallet.

DAYLIGHTING: A BRIGHT IDEA

Daylighting—using natural light from the sun to illuminate a room—lets us keep electric lights off during the day, saving energy and money. When we're inside, exposure to natural light gives us an emotional and physical connection to what's going on outside. Even if we're absorbed in an

Left and opposite: Tall windows illuminate a stairwell, while the skylight on the opposite wall balances the daylight levels. White interior surfaces help keep the hallway bright.

activity, we subconsciously register the momentary passing of a cloud or the golden tinge on the walls as the day winds down.

Exposure to daylight may even help keep our spirits up. During the short days of winter, some people experience a form of depression called Seasonal Affective Disorder, or SAD, which has been linked to daylight deprivation. People may even be more productive in daylit environments. Studies show that children in classrooms with good daylighting perform better on standardized tests than children in classrooms with little or no daylighting.

But just as some sunlight on our skin is good for us but too much is damaging, too much sun in our homes can be counterproductive. Direct sunlight streaming into a room through a clear skylight or a west-facing window can create uncomfortable glare that makes it difficult to see a TV or computer screen or even read a magazine. Too much direct sun can quickly cause a room to overheat, especially in hot climates.

Good daylighting doesn't happen by accident—it's both an art and a science. The goal is to provide plenty of balanced, glare-free natural light, while controlling the amount of heat that's lost or gained through windows and skylights, encouraging cross ventilation, and providing desirable views and connections to the outdoors.

A north exposure is generally very effective for providing good daylight. Direct beams of sunlight don't enter a room from the north, so the light is diffuse—it's bright but doesn't create uncomfortable glare. South-facing exposures can also provide good daylighting, provided there's some kind of shading device on the outside, such as a roof eave or awning, to keep the hot summer sun off the south-facing glass. A fairly small overhang over the window is usually all that's needed on the south side. This is because in the Northern Hemisphere during the summer, the sun takes a high arc through the sky, and the sun's rays hit the south side of your home at a high angle—so a

> Good daylighting doesn't happen by accident—it's both an art and a science.

Above left and right: In hot climates, large skylights can sometimes introduce too much heat into a home. In this living room, a small tubular skylight brings in daylight without the heat.

Left: Eight skylights—four on either side of the roof ridge—brighten this second-floor landing and loft. White interior surfaces help spread the light.

Opposite: Well-designed windows and skylights suffuse this bathroom with natural light. The lower portions of some windows are sandblasted for privacy. A window near the ceiling (top left) opens to allow rising warm air to escape.

fairly narrow overhang provides adequate shade. In the winter, when getting more heat in the home is desirable in most regions, the sun is at a lower angle and will penetrate farther into a south-facing room.

The west façade is the most difficult orientation for daylighting because west-facing windows let in the hot afternoon sun, which may overheat your home. Use as few west-facing windows as possible, unless you're in a cold northern climate where you want as much heat as you can get.

GOOD **GREEN** RECOMMENDATIONS:
DAYLIGHTING

■ *In cold climates*, use fewer windows on the building's colder north side. Use double-pane, low-e windows with a **U**-factor of 0.35 or below (to keep heat inside your home) and a solar heat gain coefficient of 0.60 or higher (to allow more of the sun's heat to enter your home).

■ *In temperate climates*, use fewer windows on the west side. On south-facing windows, a simple overhang or awning will allow plenty of natural light in while keeping out the summer's heat.

■ *In hot and arid climates* with intense sunlight, such as the Southwest, avoid west-facing windows if possible. Design windows to let in indirect daylight rather than direct beams of sunlight. Consider shading options such as deep eaves, verandas, awnings, exterior shutters, and deciduous trees and vines. Use low-e windows specifically designed for hot climates, with a solar heat gain coefficient of 0.40 or less (**U**-factor is less important than SHGC in hot regions).

■ *In hot and humid climates* such as the Southeast, position windows on two sides of a room to improve cross ventilation. A skylight that opens or a window placed high on a wall can provide a path for hot air to flow out of your house. Use exterior shading strategies to keep direct sun off all windows.

■ *Bring in light from above* with clerestories or skylights. Clerestories, which are windows placed high on the wall, often above the main roofline, allow daylight to penetrate deep into a room. If you're installing skylights, consider models with translucent or prismatic glazing so the light from above is diffuse rather than uncomfortably bright. Also consider tubular skylights, which are small circular skylights at the end of a reflective tube. They're less expensive to install than regular skylights, and they make a good retrofit solution for existing homes.

■ *Reduce glare* by daylighting rooms from more than one side. For example, if large view windows dominate one side of a room, placing a row of small clerestory windows high on the opposite wall will help balance the light.

■ *Take advantage of indirect daylight* by using light-colored interior surfaces, including walls, ceilings, floor coverings, and furnishings. Light surfaces reflect daylight, making the room brighter. Splayed window reveals and splayed skylight wells, especially if they're painted white, also help spread daylight farther into a room. A window located close to a room's corner will also help spread daylight by illuminating the wall that's perpendicular to the window.

■ *Think of windows as holes in your wall.* Even with high-performance glazing, skylights and windows act a bit like holes in your walls—they're much less effective at keeping heat in or out of your home than insulated walls are. If you're remodeling or building a new home, be judicious with the size, number, and placement of windows and skylights.

EFFICIENT ELECTRIC LIGHTING

Daylighting isn't the solution all the time, of course. But thanks to advances in lighting technology, there are attractive *and* energy-efficient options for brightening our homes on gloomy days and after the sun goes down.

Fluorescent lights use a third to a quarter of the electricity of standard incandescent bulbs (what most of us consider regular light bulbs). And fluorescent lights last up to ten times longer. If you still associate fluorescent lighting with those old humming tubes that gave off a greenish cast, take a new look at today's fluorescent lights.

> Take a new look at today's fluorescent lights.

The current generation of light fixtures that use linear fluorescent bulbs (or tubes) don't flicker or hum as in the old days. Linear fluorescent fixtures are most often used in kitchens and bathrooms. In addition, there's a newer type of fluorescent light—the compact fluorescent light bulb, or CFL, which comes in a variety of shapes and sizes. CFLs screw into most light fixtures designed for a regular bulb, including table and floor lamps, sconces, and recessed ceiling lights. CFLs, which are sold by most home improvement stores, are usually labeled "warm white" or "cool white." The warm-white CFLs give off a light comparable to regular (incandescent) bulbs.

CFLs cost more than regular bulbs, but over the life of the bulb you can save as much as $60—you'll see the greatest savings if you use them in locations where the light is usually left on for fifteen minutes or more at a time. CFLs are great for hard-to-reach locations because they last eight to ten times longer than regular bulbs, and your home will stay cooler because they give off little heat. However, some compact fluorescent bulbs can't be used with dimmers, in outdoor fixtures in cold climates, or in enclosed indoor fixtures—so read the package before purchasing them.

> CFLs cost more than regular bulbs, but over the life of the bulb you can save as much as $60.

Lighting controls such as automatic timers, motion sensors, and photocontrols can cut your energy use and add a little convenience to your life. If you leave lights on for security when you're not home, put automatic timers on table or floor lamps so the bulbs aren't burning all day long. For exterior lights, consider installing a motion sensor so the light only comes on when someone approaches. Or put in a photocell control so the light comes on at dusk and goes off automatically in the morning.

Halogen lights are a type of incandescent bulb that produces a bright white light suitable for accent lighting, such as highlighting artwork. They're somewhat more efficient than regular incandescent bulbs but not nearly as efficient as CFLs, so use them sparingly. Avoid high-wattage halogen torchieres, which can get as hot as 1,000 degrees Fahrenheit, creating a potential fire hazard and squandering energy. A low-wattage fluorescent torchiere will provide comparable light quality while keeping your home cooler and reducing your energy bill by as much as $50 each year.

COMFORT ZONE:
SMART ENERGY USE FOR BETTER LIVING

How comfortable you feel in your home depends on a range of factors: air temperature, relative humidity, air movement, the materials your home is made of, and even the clothes you're wearing. The most effective way to keep your home comfortable is to rely on passive means: orienting your home to take advantage of the sun's warmth, shading it to keep it cool, positioning windows to take advantage of cooling breezes, and using building materials that keep heat in or out, depending on the season.

In most places, however, there are times when passive measures aren't up to the task of keeping you comfortable, and you'll want mechanical heating or cooling to kick in. If a home is well designed for natural heating and cooling, the mechanical equipment will essentially be a backup system that won't have to run as often or as long.

NATURAL HEATING AND COOLING

A comfortable energy-efficient home doesn't require complicated high-tech solutions. Our grandparents and the generations before them knew how to build homes that would be livable year round without depending on vast amounts of fuel. New England saltbox-style houses turned their backs to the cold northern wind, with steeply pitched roofs angling low toward the ground to deflect winds. In the days before air conditioning, many houses in the Southeast were built with wide wraparound verandas and louvered shutters that kept hot sun off the house while allowing in cooling cross-breezes. In modest Southern dogtrot homes, a covered breezeway separated the home's two rooms, channeling cooling breezes and creating a shady area for doing household chores.

In hot arid climates like the American Southwest, shade is precious. A porch roof of corrugated metal keeps sun off the windows.

Creating a good green home entails first working *with* nature—making your home as responsive as you can to the local climate. The next step is to supplement that well-designed home with regionally appropriate, energy-efficient technology. The results? A comfortable home that saves money and the planet's resources year after year.

The two most common approaches to climate-responsive design are *passive solar heating* and *natural cooling*. Passive solar heating means using the sun's warmth to heat your home. When properly done, it can reduce a typical

[A comfortable energy-efficient home doesn't require complicated high-tech solutions.]

home's need for heating by 30 to 50 percent. It's most effective in cold sunny regions and in regions where there's a big temperature difference from day to night. But it can be used to good effect even in cloudy, temperate zones. Natural cooling uses shading and breezes to cool a home. It's effective just about everywhere, although in extremely hot or humid climates it usually needs to be supplemented with air conditioning for at least some of the year.

If you're building a new home, you'll have more leeway to incorporate natural heating and cooling strategies. But even with existing homes, you may be able to make some changes to enhance passive solar heating and natural cooling.

GOOD GREEN RECOMMENDATIONS: NATURAL HEATING AND COOLING

■ *South-facing windows for winter heating.* For passive solar heating, the goal is to allow in the sun's heat during the colder months while keeping it out during hot times of the year. To achieve this, it's best to orient the home so that its longest wall faces south. The south façade should have the most windows, with fewer windows on the east and north sides. The hot west side should have as few windows as possible, except in very cold climates where you want as much heat as you can get. The optimum size and location of your windows will depend on your climate.

■ *Thermal mass for retaining the sun's warmth.* If you live in a cold sunny climate, or a climate with hot days and cool nights, you can take advantage of thermal mass to store the sun's warmth in your home. If you've ever stood next to a boulder or a concrete building after nightfall and felt warmth coming off its surface, that's thermal mass at work: the massive material has been absorbing the sun's heat during the day, and now is radiating that warmth to the cooler air. Ceramic tile or concrete floors make excellent collectors of the sun's heat as long as they aren't

covered with carpet. Massive stone fireplaces or thick earthen walls are also quite effective. Even a double layer of drywall on wood-framed walls can add considerable thermal mass.

■ *Keeping the heat out.* If you live in a warm climate where temperatures don't cool off much at night, a thermally massive building isn't the best approach. Instead, use shading, cross-ventilation, a white roof, and appropriate insulation to keep your home cool. Consider wide verandas and covered porches, roofs with deep eaves, awnings, or trellises. Plant deciduous trees that will shade the building in the summer and drop their leaves in the winter to let in more of the sun's warmth.

■ *Cooling breezes.* Take advantage of breezes and air movement to cool your home. Rooms should have operable windows on more than one wall to encourage cross ventilation. Casement and louvered windows do a better job of allowing in breezes because they can be fully opened. Double-hung, single-hung, and horizontal sliding windows are somewhat less effective. A clerestory window or skylight that opens will allow hot air that's risen to the ceiling to escape from the home.

NATURALLY COOL

Modern architecture is sometimes associated with an attitude that puts style before comfort, elevating the architect's vision above the needs of the people who live in the building. Not so in this house in Venice, California, designed for his family by David Hertz, an architect who brings together modernist and environmentalist sensibilities.

Underneath this home's sexy modern skin, it's all about efficiency. The design makes good use of the 40 x 90-foot urban lot, accommodating a 2,700-square-foot house, a garage, and a surprisingly generous amount of usable outdoor space. Inside, there are no "museum" rooms—those formal living and dining rooms and grand foyers that see little use but gobble up square footage. The house is energy and resource efficient, too. It makes

> **[Underneath this home's sexy modern skin, it's all about efficiency.]**

Located about a half mile from the Pacific Ocean, this house is naturally cooled, heated, and lit much of the time. It's a durable, low-maintenance house, built with rugged materials that will hold up over time and withstand energetic handling by three active children.

Right: A tall slot window in the children's bathroom provides privacy while letting in light. The bathroom surfaces are Syndecrete, a concrete solid-surfacing material developed by Hertz. Syndecrete is a mix of cement and recycled materials, including fly ash (a waste product from coal-burning electric utilities), glass, reground plastic, and scrap metal. Hertz also used Syndecrete for the kitchen counters, fireplace, and much of the furniture in the house.

Above: A jumble of our society's junk brightens a particularly colorful Syndecrete tile.

Below: With a concrete floor, there's no need to use additional resources like wood, tile, or carpet for a finish flooring.

the most of the sun's free energy for heating, cooling, and lighting, while incorporating recycled materials within a durable low-maintenance structure.

The home is split into two sections linked by a second-story bridge. In the front portion, the kitchen, dining, living, and family areas are arranged in a flowing U-shape. Above the main living areas are the master bedroom, master bath, and study. A sun-drenched interior bridge crosses from the master bedroom over an outdoor courtyard to the rear structure, where the children's two bedrooms flank a bathroom. Beneath the children's

A sun-splashed bridge crosses from the master bedroom to the children's wing. Beneath is an open-air courtyard for playing and barbecuing. One wall of the bridge is clad with Syndecrete tiles. It faces south, serving as a passive solar collector that stores the sun's heat and radiates it back into the home when temperatures cool. When the interior temperature rises to a certain point, a high window and two skylights automatically open to draw hot air from the house.

Right: There's little wasted space—even the flat roof is put to work. The master bedroom opens onto an outdoor living room. Further back on the roof there's a hot tub, a solar water heater, a sunny lounging area, and an orchid greenhouse. The building's exterior is almost 50 percent glass, yet Hertz says it's still very energy efficient, in part because he used high-performance windows and sky-lights that block heat gain and loss.

rooms is a garage accessible from a rear alley.

Many of the rooms borrow light, views, and space from each other, giving the home an airy feel. An open staircase and a loft-like study keep the upstairs and downstairs connected, while strategically placed windows provide views and fresh air from one end of the house to the other.

The home was designed to be comfortable without air conditioning. Upstairs, hopper windows channel cooling Pacific Ocean breezes from the master bedroom across the bridge to the children's rooms. A transom window above the bedroom door allows cross ventilation even when the door is closed. Warm air from down-stairs rises up the open staircase and is flushed out through a high window and two skylights that automatically open when the temperature reaches a certain point. The high-performance skylights have a special mirrored film between two panes of glass, blocking heat gain while allowing in plenty of daylight.

Concrete floors provide excellent thermal mass, absorbing the sun's heat during the day and slowly radiating that heat back into the living spaces in the

When the afternoon sun hits the front of the house (bottom left), light slices through the glass gaps in the poured-in-place concrete wall and bench (left and bottom right). Hydronic radiant-heating pipes run through the concrete floor, the bench, and even the showers. A rooftop solar collector heats water, providing about 80 percent of the family's space heating and hot water needs, with a gas-fired water heater making up the difference.

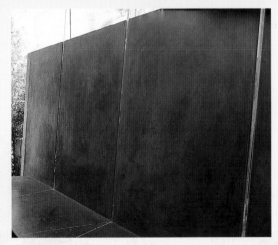

evening when temperatures drop. Shading is also used to good advantage. A second-story deck shades the windows below, while bamboo and other plants close to the house provide additional cooling. Despite being in a residential neighborhood that's densely built up, the home feels surprisingly connected to the natural environment—thanks to the flow of ocean breezes, the warmth of sunlit rooms, and the lively interplay of indoor and outdoor spaces.

HEATING AND COOLING SYSTEMS

If you plan to install new heating or cooling equipment in your home, buy energy-efficient models—they'll keep you comfortable while reducing your energy bills year after year. Many of the more efficient products carry the Energy Star label.

In the United States, 84 percent of homes have central heating, and by far the most common system is the forced-air furnace. If you're in the market for a new furnace, select one with an efficiency of 90 percent or greater. If you're going to be purchasing a new central air conditioning system, look for one with a Seasonal Energy Efficiency Ratio (SEER) of thirteen or higher (SEER is a measure of the system's energy efficiency). If you're buying a room air conditioning unit, look for Energy Star–labeled products and select a unit that's not oversized for the space you're going to cool.

If you're replacing heating or cooling equipment or selecting a system for a new home, make sure that the contractor does an accurate load calculation to ensure that the equipment and ducts are properly sized for your house. Many builders routinely install larger systems than necessary, often because that's less complicated than selecting equipment tailored to each home's specific needs. An overly large heating or air conditioning system won't make you more comfortable. In fact, it may make you less comfortable because it will cycle on and off more frequently. It also may be noisier and produce uncomfortably hot or cold drafts. An oversized system also means that you'll pay too much up front for the equipment, and too much for energy over the system's life.

If you're building a new home, consider installing a heating or air conditioning system with zones, so that you can regulate the temperature in different areas of your home depending on how you're using the rooms. Another way to get greater savings from a new or existing heating or cooling system is to

COOL ROOFS

If you live in a hot climate, consider installing a "cool roof." Cool roof materials are reflective—typically white or light-colored—and have a high emissivity, meaning they're able to shed heat readily. For homes, white metal and white tile are among the most effective cool-roof materials. A white roof reflects much of the sun's heat away, keeping the attic as much as 25 to 30 degrees Fahrenheit cooler and reducing energy use and air conditioning bills.

Besides making individual homes hotter, dark roofs contribute to the urban "heat island" effect: they absorb heat during the day and release it at night, raising a city's air temperature by up to 8 degrees Fahrenheit. This leads to more air conditioning use, resulting in more pollution from power plants.

The U.S. Environmental Protection Agency's Energy Star program certifies many roofing products that keep roofs cooler.

The owners of this home on Bainbridge Island, near Seattle, opted for an in-floor radiant heating system because it provides gentle, quiet, draft-free warmth. Hot water circulates in tubes laid below the bamboo floor, and the system is zoned to allow the temperature to vary in different rooms. For homes that need central air conditioning, a forced-air system is usually a better option than radiant heating since the furnace and air conditioner can share the ductwork.

install an electronic thermostat that allows you to program separate settings for weekdays and weekends, so that you aren't wasting energy when you're sleeping or away from home. To keep the furnace or air conditioner working efficiently, be sure to clean or replace the filters periodically (follow the manufacturer's recommendation).

Central air conditioning is becoming almost as prevalent in new homes as central heating

already is. But in climates that aren't extremely hot or humid, a whole-house fan may provide ample comfort during the summer at a substantially lower cost. A whole-house fan provides ventilation and cooling by drawing air in from open windows and expelling it through the attic and roof. And in many regions, ceiling fans, combined with good cross-breezes, may be all you need to stay comfortable during warmer months. Even if you still need air conditioning for cooling or dehumidification, ceiling fans can help reduce the amount of air conditioning energy you use. In the winter, ceiling fans can be used in rooms with high ceilings to push warm air down.

A ceiling fan can save money and energy by reducing the need for air conditioning. Ceiling fans make people feel more comfortable but they don't actually cool the air, so turn them off when no one is in the room. Not all fans are created equal. Look for Energy Star fans that are about 20 percent more efficient than average.

STOPPING AIR LEAKS

Heated or cooled air (called "conditioned" air) leaking out of your home, and outside "unconditioned" air leaking into your home, are major sources of discomfort and high energy bills. In some homes, these leaks can allow a home's entire volume of air to escape as frequently as every hour.

It's common in single-family houses for the heating and cooling ductwork to run through unconditioned spaces such as attics, crawl spaces, and uninsulated basements. But here's the problem: ducts lose a great deal of their heating and cooling energy to those unconditioned spaces. If ducts were perfectly sealed and extremely well insulated, this wouldn't be a big concern. Unfortunately, ducts are often sloppily installed or develop separations at their joints over the years, and those leaks allow conditioned air to escape.

[Ducts are often sloppily installed or develop separations at their joints.]

If you're building a new home, one alternative is to locate the ductwork within the home's conditioned space (in a dropped ceiling area, for example, or within an attic that's conditioned). If your home has ducts running through an unconditioned area, make sure all duct joints are connected and well sealed with a mastic sealant. (Don't use duct tape! Duct tape is great for a lot of purposes, but ironically, not for sealing ducts.) In most climates, ducts should also be insulated.

> Sealing unnecessary leaks can reduce cooling and heating bills by 10 percent or more.

Cracks and gaps around doors and windows, and holes around pipes and vents that pass through walls, also waste energy and can make a home uncomfortable. These openings can allow moist air to get into places it shouldn't be, such as insulated wall and ceiling cavities, where it can condense and cause mold and rot. You don't want to totally seal your house—it's important to use your bathroom and kitchen exhaust fans, for example, to draw moisture out of your home to help prevent mold growth. But sealing unnecessary leaks can reduce cooling and heating bills by 10 percent or more. Reduce air leakage by installing weather stripping around doors and windows and caulking holes around pipes and vents.

INSULATION

Insulating your home—lining the floors, walls, and ceiling with materials that block the flow of heat into or out of your house—makes your home quieter and more comfortable, saves energy, and cuts your heating and cooling bills. Insulation's effectiveness is indicated by its R-value, which is a measurement of the material's resistance to heat flow. Higher R-values provide more insulation.

Because heat rises, it's more likely to escape through the roof than the walls or floor, so in most climates higher levels of insulation are used above the ceiling than in other parts of the home. How much to use and where to install it is climate- and site-dependent. For new construction, local building codes generally require certain minimum levels of insulation but it's often worthwhile to exceed that.

There are four basic types of insulation: fiberglass, mineral wool, cellulose, and foam:

Fiberglass. In the United States, about 90 percent of homes are insulated with fiberglass. It's available in rolls or batts that are set between framing studs or joists, or as loose fill that's blown into wall cavities or attics. Some fiberglass products contain 30 percent or more recycled glass. Consider using fiberglass insulation designed to reduce discomfort during installation or potential health risks. These include formaldehyde-free products, batts wrapped in plastic to

GOOD GREEN RECOMMENDATIONS: ENERGY-EFFICIENT APPLIANCES

■ *Refrigerators and freezers.* Refrigerators and freezers, with their 24/7 operating mode, have long been real energy hogs. A typical refrigerator from the mid-1970s, with automatic defrost and a top-mounted freezer, can cost nearly $170 a year to keep plugged in. Fortunately, new models are available that are dramatically more efficient—some use as little as one-fifth the amount of electricity that refrigerators used thirty years ago. Not all new models are equally efficient, though. The yellow EnergyGuide label can help you compare the energy use and operating costs of various models. In general, larger refrigerators use more energy than smaller ones. Certain features increase energy use, such as side-by-side doors, automatic icemakers, and through-door dispensers. If you have more than one refrigerator or freezer in your home, think about whether that extra capacity is really worth it—if it's an older model, it could be costing you a hefty chunk of change each year.

■ *Clothes washers, clothes dryers, and dishwashers.* New energy-smart models are available that use substantially less water and energy. Look for the yellow EnergyGuide label to compare efficiencies.

Front-loading washing machines (also called horizontal axis) can reduce water use by up to 40 percent and energy use by up to 50 percent compared to top-loading models. Some new clothes dryers have sensors that automatically turn off the machine when clothes are dry.

■ *Computers and home entertainment equipment.* Enable the energy-saving feature on your computers so that they automatically go into "sleep" mode after a period of inactivity. Turn computers off when you won't be using them for a few hours, and turn off peripherals such as printers and scanners when you're not using them. Keep in mind that many electronic devices—such as mobile phone chargers, TVs, DVD players, stereos and other equipment with a transformer box, a remote, a clock, or memory—continue to draw electricity even when you aren't using them. These energy "leaks" or "phantom loads" can account for nearly 10 percent of your electricity bill. Either plug the devices in when you need to use them and unplug them when done—or put them on a switched outlet that can be turned on and off as needed.

reduce the installer's contact with the fibers, and products formulated so that the glass fibers don't readily break off.

Mineral wool or rock wool is similar to fiberglass, except that it's made from furnace slag or rocks that are melted and then spun to form fibers. It's available as loose fill, batts, or rolls.

Cellulose insulation typically contains 75 percent or more recycled newspaper, has no added formaldehyde, and is treated with a nontoxic chemical to make it insect, fire, and mold resistant. Damp-spray cellulose, a damp mix of cellulose and binders that is sprayed between wall studs before hanging drywall, does an excellent job of filling nooks and crannies and reducing air leaks. Loose-fill cellulose, which is blown into wall cavities and attics, can be an effective retrofit solution for older homes.

Foam insulation comes in two types: rigid sheets and foamed-in-place. Rigid sheets are used over wall studs, on cathedral ceilings and basement walls, and in many other ways. Foamed-in-place insulation is sprayed between wall studs or joists. It immediately expands and sets, effectively sealing air gaps and providing excellent insulation. Excess foam that expands beyond the studs can be shaved off.

Another type of product called a *radiant barrier* isn't actually an insulator, but it can be very effective at stopping heat from entering your home. Radiant barriers are made of a reflective material, essentially an aluminum foil, applied to a substrate such as kraft paper, plastic film, plywood, or oriented strand board. It's usually used in attics in hot climates, with the reflective surface installed so that it faces an air space to block transfer of radiant heat into the home. In the winter, radiant barriers can also reduce some heat loss from the home, but their main benefit is their ability to block summer heat gain.

WATER HEATING

With a conventional water heater, water is heated in a tank and held there until you're ready to use it. But the water in the tank cools off and has to be continually reheated to maintain the set water temperature. Fifteen percent of a water heater's energy can be lost this way. Wrapping the tank with an insulating jacket can help, as can purchasing a more energy-efficient model (keep in mind that gas water heaters are substantially more energy efficient than electric models). Also consider lowering the thermostat setting on your water heater: 120 degrees Fahrenheit is usually sufficiently hot. You may also want to consider alternative systems, such as an instantaneous or demand (tankless) water heater that heats water as you need it, or a solar water heater.

[Consider lowering the thermostat setting on your water heater.]

Solar water heaters, also called solar-thermal systems, are different from the solar power systems used to create electricity. Instead, solar water heaters absorb the sun's heat and transfer it to water that is then used for regular household needs, swimming pools and spas, and sometimes for heating rooms.

A typical system used for heating household water consists of one or more collectors (usually a glass-topped insulated box that contains a black metal panel designed to absorb heat). The collectors are typically mounted on a roof and angled to face south. Liquid circulates in

Rooftop solar collectors on this house preheat water for regular household use and for a radiant-floor heating system.

tubes through the collectors, where it heats up when the sun is shining. In some systems, the liquid is potable water that's stored in a tank until needed. In other systems, the liquid is an antifreeze solution that flows through a heat exchanger to heat your potable water.

Solar water heaters are often used to preheat a household's water, supplemented by a conventional water heater so that there's plenty of hot water first thing in the morning and during stretches of cloudy weather. If your household uses a lot of hot water, and you live in a place where there's ample sunshine and high energy costs, solar water heating can be very cost effective.

THE BEAUTY OF BUILDING GREEN

Building green needn't compromise style and graciousness, as this Northern California home so elegantly demonstrates. Completed in 1999, it was designed by the late Joseph Esherick and architect Cathy Schwabe, in collaboration with the home's owner, Sandra Slater, a designer and sustainable-building consultant. The property, located about thirty miles south of San Francisco in Palo Alto, previously housed an auto body shop. It's on a transitional block between a tranquil residential neighborhood and a bustling commercial and retail district, within walking and bicycling distance of shops, restaurants, and neighborhood services.

The 2,900-square-foot home consists of two wings joined by a light-filled stairwell and second-story bridge. The heart of the home—an open great room and kitchen on the ground floor—is angled south to take advantage of daylight. Above this space is the master suite with a generous deck. The other wing houses two bedrooms and a bath downstairs, with a bedroom, bath, laundry, and deck above.

Located in a temperate climate, the home was designed

Spectrally selective low-e glass on the south- and west-facing windows blocks some of the sun's heat in the summer and reduces heat loss inside the home in the winter. Overhangs and trellises keep heat out while allowing in daylight.

to be comfortable without air conditioning. Vine-covered trellises, roof overhangs, and low-e windows help keep the home cool in the summer. Fresh air flows into the home through windows at lower levels, while hot air rises upstairs and flows out through windows positioned near the ceiling's peak.

The house was built using advanced wood-framing techniques, including studs spaced twenty-four inches apart instead of the more conventional sixteen-inch spacing. This reduced

Above: This sensuous sink was fashioned from Honduran mahogany certified to have come from a sustainably managed forest.

Top right: A stairwell wrapped in glass draws in daylight. The stairs and handrail are made of certified sustainably harvested jarrah, a beautifully grained Australian eucalyptus.

Below right: A special fireplace grate burns wood efficiently, reducing emissions and radiating more heat into the home than a conventional wood-burning fireplace. The fireplace surround is constructed of steel stair treads salvaged from a school. The home is heated with a radiant-floor heating system that has six zones, so that it can be turned off in unoccupied rooms, saving energy and money.

wood use by about 10 percent. The structure also includes recycled steel beams, engineered laminated beams that make efficient use of small-diameter trees, and wood certified by the Forest Stewardship Council to have come from sustainably harvested forests. In the wall and ceiling cavities, cellulose insulation made from recycled newspapers keeps the home comfortable and quiet.

On top of the detached garage, photovoltaic (PV) panels capture the sun's energy and convert it to electricity, meeting about 30 to 40 percent of the home's electricity needs in the winter and about 75 percent during the summer. From Sandra's perspective, the integration of the PV system, the utility grid, and her home's electrical system is seamless, requiring no maintenance or tending on her part other than occasionally hosing dust and leaves off the panels. Sandra calculated that the green features added 4.5 percent to the cost of building her home, but she expects to recoup that expense within ten years, thanks to lower utility bills.

Above and below right: Bamboo flooring, usually blond, is here stained a deeper color. Using bamboo, a fast-growing grass, reduces demand for slower-growing, more ecologically sensitive tree species. Cabinets are FSC-certified cherry wood.

Below left: The concrete mix used for the front walk includes fly ash, a waste product from coal-burning electric utilities. Blue recycled-glass cullet adds sparkle. A concrete pad inside the patio door received the same treatment.

SOLAR POWER:
IT'S CLEAN, IT'S GREEN, IT'S HERE

A good green home is an energy-efficient home. It's well insulated and weather-proofed. It's illuminated with daylight and energy-efficient electric lighting. It takes advantage of climate-appropriate strategies, such as passive solar heating and natural cooling, supplemented by efficient mechanical systems.

Once you've got those green building blocks in place, consider taking the greening of your home a step further by harnessing the sun's energy to generate electricity. Using solar power is an exciting, rewarding way to kick the addiction to fossil fuels without sacrificing the comforts and quality of life we're accustomed to. Photovoltaic cells, also known as solar cells, convert sunlight into electricity. They're a clean source of energy that's becoming increasingly attractive to homeowners, thanks in part to government-sponsored incentives and programs that allow homeowners to get credit on their utility bills for excess electricity that their PV system sends back to the electricity grid.

If you're considering going solar, first do what you can to make your home energy efficient. There's little sense installing a solar electricity system if your home's going to squander that energy. Then take into account your home's location and orientation. To make solar worthwhile, you'll want good southern exposure, ample sunny days, and an unobstructed shadow-free rooftop or other area where the system can be installed.

In this suburban San Diego development, PV panels on top of a backyard trellis generate up to 2.4 kilowatts of electricity from the sun. That won't meet all the energy demands of a large home, but it's enough to make a sizable dent in monthly electricity bills. A special meter (top) shows how much electricity the panels are producing and how much the home is using at any given moment.

PHOTOVOLTAICS: MAKING ELECTRICITY FROM SUNLIGHT

Solar-energy systems typically consist of individual PV cells grouped into panels that produce direct current (DC) electricity rather than the alternating current (AC) electricity we use in our homes. A device called an inverter converts the DC to AC electricity. PV panels can be mounted on your roof or on the ground. They should face south and be pitched at an angle to best capture sunlight, in a location where buildings or trees won't cast shadows on them.

In remote areas, it can be less expensive to install a PV system than to run utility wires a great distance to the home. Increasingly, PV panels are also turning up in households that are already hooked into the electric utility network. Many states have instituted a program called *net metering,* which allows homeowners to link their PV systems to the local utility grid. When the PV system is generating more electricity than the household is using, the excess electricity feeds into the utility grid, spinning the electricity meter backward. When the household requires more electricity than the PV system is generating, the household draws energy from the utility grid.

Even with net metering, PV electricity may not yet be cost competitive with electricity provided by your utility company. But given concerns about pollution and about national security issues related to fossil fuel consumption, PV power is certain to play an increasingly important role in our future.

At Civano, a sustainably developed master-planned community in Tucson, homes have solar water-heating systems that supply most of the required hot water in the summer. Gas or electric water heaters provide backup water heating. In addition, SolarBuilt, one of the community's four builders, offers homes powered in part by PV systems that turn sunlight into electricity. The PV arrays shown here are mounted on garages located along alleys behind the homes. Panels face south and are angled to maximize their exposure to the sun.

GOOD GREEN AFFORDABLE HOUSING

Green building—energy efficiency, smart resource use, healthy indoor spaces—isn't yet standard practice in the home building industry, but it's getting there. Today, good green home design is making inroads everywhere, from high-end custom homes to master-planned developments to buildings such as Colorado Court, a single-room occupancy apartment complex in southern California.

Located in downtown Santa Monica on a high-visibility corner, the 44-unit building turns heads with its industrial finishes and assertive design. The most attention-grabbing feature is the 204 shimmering blue PV panels draped over the roof and southwest façade. This PV system, in conjunction with a natural gas-powered turbine/heat-recovery system on the roof, is expected to generate enough electricity to meet the bulk of the building's energy needs.

While the building's flashy PV system attracts attention, other less sexy green features are quietly doing their job. To better take advantage of natural cooling and daylighting, the studio apartments are clustered into three small towers that form a U-shape, with breezeways and open-air corridors and stairways to encourage airflow. In each apartment, high-performance operable windows provide daylight and cooling breezes, helping to keep the interiors comfortable without air conditioning.

> [While the building's flashy PV system attracts attention, other less sexy green features are quietly doing their job.]

Recycled cellulose insulation, energy-efficient lighting and appliances, draft-free radiant heating, and carefully chosen interior finishes provide the residents with a comfortable, healthy, and environmentally sustainable place to call home.

Above: Shimmering blue PV panels wrap the roof and façade of this apartment complex.

Opposite: The building's high-tech green features are complemented by low-tech approaches. Breezeways between the buildings encourage airflow, while the apartments' operable windows let in daylight and capture cooling breezes, eliminating the need for air conditioning.

Left: The single-room-occupancy apartments for low-income residents are modest—about 375 square feet—but designed to be healthy and comfortable. Windows are double-pane, low-e, and filled with krypton gas for superior insulation, while wall cavities are filled with insulation made from recycled newspapers. Compact fluorescent lights and energy-efficient appliances reduce energy use. Cabinets are made with formaldehyde-free medium-density fiberboard. On the floor, real linoleum—a blend of linseed oil, sawdust, pigments and other natural materials—is used in the kitchen area, entry, and bathroom, with recycled-content carpet elsewhere.

build for
TODAY
and tomorrow

A building is an intricate system with interdependent parts. It has a complex skin (the building envelope) that's both resilient and fragile, generally capable of protecting us from the elements but vulnerable to damage. Like a body, a building takes in nutrients (sunlight, electricity, gas, water) that give it energy. It also produces waste—combustion byproducts, outgassed chemicals, polluted water. It breathes in fresh air, moisture vapor, and contaminants from the outside, and it breathes out stale air, moisture vapor, and contaminants from within. It looks downtrodden when neglected. It glows when loved.

The more you learn about how your home functions as a system, the more successful you'll be at creating a place that will give as much satisfaction 100 years from now as it does today. Not all of us, however, have the time or inclination to become an expert in building design and construction. Fortunately, there are experienced building professionals out there—builders, architects, contractors, interior designers, tradespeople—who are passionate about creating homes of lasting value. Whether you're remodeling, buying a home, or building from scratch, seek out building professionals you can trust for sensible advice and quality workmanship.

Right: Low-maintenance, durable exterior materials—including fiber-cement siding (above right), a standing-seam metal roof (page 88), and a deck built with composite lumber that blends wood waste and recycled plastic (above left)—will help make this home last. South-facing windows and a passive solar design mean it uses less energy for lighting and heating. Additional energy-savvy measures include compact fluorescent lights and water- and energy-conserving appliances. Inside, careful attention was paid to using equipment, products, and finishes that contribute to good indoor air quality, including a hydronic radiant-floor heating system and zero-VOC paints. The owner estimates that green features added less than 1 percent to the entire budget, while the benefits—energy efficiency, comfort, good indoor air quality, and less time and money spent on maintenance—will last a lifetime.

What makes a home last? Smart design and quality construction that embrace the art *and* the science of building. Construction methods and building materials that are climate appropriate—that hold up to heat, freezing temperatures, rain, wind, earthquakes, or whatever your regional challenges are. A design that's flexible—one that people find appealing and livable today and that can be readily adapted to changing needs, changing life stages, and changing demographics.

This metal roof is lightweight, strong, and durable. The metal panels contain recycled content and are recyclable.

GOOD GREEN RECOMMENDATIONS: BUILD FOR TODAY AND TOMORROW

■ *Does your home incorporate universal design?* Is your home user-friendly for a variety of people—children, the elderly, people with diverse physical abilities? Will you have to remodel or move if you can no longer climb stairs, reach high cabinets, or step into a bathtub? Ideally, universal design principles should be built into our homes from the outset, but they may also be incorporated into remodeling and repair projects. Grab bars in the bathroom are one example of universal design, as are sinks and cooktops that can be used by a person in a wheelchair. Many universal design strategies make life easier for all of us. Something as simple as replacing round doorknobs with lever handles can make a big difference, whether you have arthritis or just have your hands full.

■ *Is the building tough?* Will it age gracefully or is it made with poor quality or climate-inappropriate materials that will warp, rot, splinter, or otherwise give out? Pay attention to the details that matter. Proper drainage around the site, for example, is ultimately more important than the style of porch light you select.

■ *Is it easy to maintain?* There's no such thing as a maintenance-free home, but some materials require less upkeep than others do. Use siding that doesn't require painting every five years, decking that will last through your children's childhood, and flooring that's a snap to clean and won't need frequent replacement.

■ *Is it easy to live with?* Is the building energy-smart so that it's comfortable and costs less to live in? Is it aesthetically pleasing so that you want to spend time in it and take care of it? Is it easy for the neighbors to live with? Or does the kitchen window look into the neighbor's bedroom, is every bit of earth paved over, are all the trees cut down?

■ *Will the building evolve?* An adaptable building is more likely to endure for generations. Think of a brick warehouse converted into artists' lofts, an abandoned high school reconfigured into modern condos, or a city mansion carved into gracious flats.

TALKING TRASH

Building a 2,000-square-foot home generates almost thirteen tons of waste—wood, concrete, gypsum, and a host of other materials. Back when land and natural resources seemed unlimited, it was easier and often cheaper to toss the debris rather than find a use for it. That's changing as people realize we can't keep throwing things away—because there is no "away."

Three strategies can make a big dent in the trash heap our home-building industry creates. The first step is to reuse existing buildings. Assuming a building is structurally sound, it can be reused, remodeled, or even moved to another site rather than be demolished.

If you own a building that's too far gone to be reused, consider dismantling instead of razing it. Siding, framing lumber, windows, doors, flooring, lighting fixtures, plumbing fixtures, cabinets, trim—it's all valuable material that can be put to good use in your new home, sold to a building salvage company, or donated to charitable organizations.

If you have construction or demolition waste that isn't reusable, it still may be recyclable. Recycling is different from salvaging. With salvaging, the material is basically reused intact. With recycling, the material is processed into a new form, such as when newspapers are pulped and made into paper bags. Recycling options for used construction materials vary by region—in some communities it's possible to recycle drywall, metal, glass, carpet, concrete, and other materials. Check with your local waste management agency or recycling office—they will be able to tell you what's recyclable in your area. While you're at it, be sure to close the loop: Buy building products that contain recycled content to create demand for the "trash" that's coming out of construction and demolition sites.

The original home on this property was badly damaged by a mudslide and remained vacant for eighteen years. Eventually, current owner Desmond McDonald, whose father had built the original house, decided to rebuild. Rather than demolishing the compromised structure and hauling it to a landfill, Desmond and his wife Julie dismantled it and salvaged as much material as possible to build the new house. Exposed beams in the living room came from the original home's roof—nail holes from the roof sheathing can still be seen. Window and door openings were fashioned from the old framing lumber. Posts used for the deck and front door (not shown) came from beams salvaged from an apartment building that was being razed. The couple built the fireplace with rocks they scavenged from the site when digging new foundation footings.

> We can't keep throwing things away—because there is no "away."

PRESERVING THE PAST, PROTECTING THE FUTURE

Protecting the environment comes naturally to Kristin and Truman Collins, owners of this charming English cottage-style house near Portland, Oregon. They're part of the family that owns The Collins Companies, a forest-products business with timber operations in Pennsylvania, California, and Oregon. All the Collins' forests are certified to meet the criteria of the Forest Stewardship Council (FSC), an independent organization that has established international standards for sustainably managed forests.

When Kristin and Truman decided to enlarge their 2,000-square-foot home to accommodate their growing family—they had a daughter, with a baby boy on the way—there was no question that they would use as much FSC-certified wood as possible. They were also committed to remaining true to the home's original character. Built in 1936, the home is now listed on the National Register of Historic Places. Its delightful exterior features include twin leaded-glass windows in front, steeply pitched roofs, casement windows with multiple panes, and decorative half-timbering.

For their home's addition, Kristin and Truman turned to the Neil Kelly Company, a local design/build firm that was meticulous in meeting the project's historic *and* environmental goals. During the course of designing the 920-square-foot addition—two bedrooms upstairs and a family room downstairs—the scope of the remodeling grew. Ultimately, it also included updating the kitchen, restoring the main bath, and refinishing the existing hardwood floors, as well as significant upgrades to the home's heating and plumbing systems.

Virtually all the wood used in the project was FSC-certified, including the framing lumber, the kitchen cabinets, and new oak flooring. The project team paid attention to what they took out of the home as well as what they put into it. Old cabinets and appliances were donated for reuse, and the bulk of the demolition material was recycled.

All these changes helped bring the home up to today's expectations for convenience, style, and performance, which will help ensure it lasts many more generations.

Left: The remodeled kitchen includes eco-friendly features such as cabinets made with FSC-certified wood and an efficient Energy Star dishwasher. The family room addition (visible in the background) includes FSC-certified oak flooring that matches the home's original floor.

Below: What's green about this blue loo? The cabinets are made from wheatboard, a type of particleboard manufactured from wheat straw, an agricultural waste material. And these cabinets help to promote good indoor air quality, since they're free of the urea-formaldehyde resin often used to make particleboard and other pressed-wood products.

Opposite page: From the street, there's virtually no sign that this 1936 home has undergone a green renovation.

Left: The addition includes a family room on the ground floor and two bedrooms upstairs (the new wing is on either side of the chimney). The designers integrated the new wing with the existing home, matching the half-timbers adorning the facade, the steeply pitched roof, and the French doors.

A SANCTUARY, SIMPLE AND STRONG

On an island in the Puget Sound north of Seattle, an artist has built a home and studio whose beguiling simplicity gives it the feel of a stage on which a creative life is unfolding. If buildings could be said to have characters, this one would be the strong silent type. It sits quietly on sloping land, ringed by cedars, neither competing with its natural surroundings nor camouflaging its nature as a built object.

After years of dwelling in Seattle lofts, feeling energized and at times restricted by living and working in close quarters, Linda Beaumont—painter, sculptor, ceramicist, public artist—felt the pull of Whidbey Island. Eventually she bought five wooded acres there. The location was close enough to the island ferry that she could readily get into Seattle to see friends and meet the creative and business demands of her work, yet far enough from the city that it truly is a place apart.

Five years passed before she was ready to start building. On and off during those years she was able to spend time on the property, camping in an Airstream trailer parked there, getting to know the land and letting it offer her clues about how she might live on it. Steve Badanes—architect, builder, teacher, and founding member of the design/build collaborative Jersey Devil—partnered with Linda. He guided the design, offering insights gained from more than twenty-five years of designing and constructing buildings that respect people and place.

> The structure feels light and lean, its most striking feature a two-story wall of south-facing windows.

Their time spent with the land yielded a clear message: Keep the structure simple, even neutral, so as not to dominate the rich and wild beauty of the place. The inspiration to clad the building in silvery corrugated metal came from Linda's years of living in the Pacific Northwest, surrounded by the glinting sea and the silver light of overcast skies.

A 20 x 40-foot two-story rectangle forms the building's core. At the second-story level, two wings project from the east and west walls, sheltering open areas underneath. The structure feels light and lean, its most striking feature a two-story wall of south-facing windows that drenches the interior spaces with year-round daylight and winter warmth. On the ground floor,

Even with all the lights on at night, little light spills beyond this home's perimeter. Light pollution, or light trespass, occurs when outdoor light fixtures let light spill onto neighboring properties or let light escape toward the night sky. The sky glow from cities and suburbs prevents us from appreciating the glory of a star-filled sky. To reduce light pollution, use outdoor light fixtures that direct all their light downward or are shielded by overhangs, and consider installing motion sensors so the lights come on only when you need them.

the south end of the building encompasses an open living/dining/kitchen area, with the bathroom, laundry, and storage spaces occupying the north end. Upstairs, Linda's studio fills the main space, with a wing to one side containing a bedroom and sleeping porch. The other wing holds a smaller workspace with a porch of its own.

The structure is spare and tough yet its spirit is warmhearted. It provides ample space, light, and air for an artist's creativity to soar. It's as comfortable sheltering one or two people as it is embracing a group of twenty friends who gather around a table under one of the wings, sharing a meal, stories, and laughter as night settles in the forest and the building's silvery skin gleams in the moonlight.

Opposite page: The second-floor studio has ample space for Beaumont to spread her creative wings. Windows on the south side and a skylight on the north suffuse the studio with light even on the grayest days. A balcony off the second-story doors is in the works.

Above: A two-story wall of windows faces south to capture daylight and warmth, both treasured commodities in the Pacific Northwest. The passive solar design includes a concrete floor to absorb the sun's heat in the winter. The blank panel behind the wood-burning stove awaits Beaumont's mosaic work.

Left: Corrugated metal siding and a metal roof will help this live-in studio in Washington State withstand decades of downpours with minimal maintenance and no painting. Straightforward shapes with no unnecessary flourishes mean fewer materials are needed for construction and upkeep. The Airstream trailer in back serves as a guest cottage.

DO YOU NEED MORE GREEN TO BE GREEN?

Many people assume that eco-friendly homes cost a bundle. This misperception has become commonplace in part because the green-built homes that attract the most attention are often the eye-catching, big-budget custom homes built with leading-edge—some would say bleeding-edge—technologies and materials. These high-visibility homes play an important role in helping raise awareness about green building. But while environmentally responsible houses can cost more than conventional houses—some say from 2 to 5 percent more—they don't have to. If you're budget-conscious—and who isn't when it comes to buying or building a home—green building can *save* you money.

The owners of this house stayed within a tight budget by doing much of the building themselves and by keeping the home compact—it's about 1,400 square feet. Durable fiber-cement siding will help keep maintenance costs in check.

GOOD GREEN RECOMMENDATIONS: KEEPING COSTS IN CHECK

■ *Start with the basics*. Many green home precepts are inherently cost effective. Think smaller—smaller homes cost less to buy, furnish, heat, and cool. Pare down, using simpler designs that are easier and less expensive to build. Look for a home that will be durable and easy to maintain. Make each building element work harder. A concrete slab, for example, can be surfaced to serve as finish flooring, saving the cost of putting in wood, tile, or carpet.

■ *Consider the true costs*. Often we're swayed by low upfront costs rather than taking into account long-term value, but when it comes to your home, that strategy can wind up costing a bundle. If you live in Vermont and skimp on insulation, you'll pay for it year after year with higher energy bills. Whether you're replacing a roof or buying a refrigerator, consider how much it will cost you over the item's life: not just how much you'll spend initially, but how much the purchase will cost you—in energy, maintenance, and even time—over the years.

■ *Realize that some products or building methods may cost more*. Some green building techniques and materials do cost more. Certain certified wood products, for example, may be more expensive because markets for them are still developing. Labor-intensive building methods such as straw bale and rammed earth can be more expensive. To keep costs down when remodeling or building a new home, consider sticking with more conventional building methods such as wood framing. Or use your savings from one area to subsidize higher costs in another. The money you save by buying or building a smaller house, for example, can be put toward bamboo flooring or higher quality windows.

■ *Think integrated design*. Your house is a system, with each component, from the light bulbs to the roof, interacting in ways that affect your wallet, your health, and the environment. Design a tight superinsulated house and you can install smaller heating and air-conditioning equipment that costs less to buy and operate. Position your windows for good daylighting and you can keep the lights off during the day, which keeps your house cooler so your air conditioner won't have to work as hard. Integrated design takes advance planning and good coordination of your entire building team but can result in major savings.

■ *Reduce waste*. Spend less on waste-hauling fees by reducing construction waste through careful planning and recycling. If you're remodeling, reuse old cabinets, appliances, wood, and other building materials—or sell or donate what you can't reuse.

■ *Look into incentive programs and special mortgages*. Many local government agencies and utility companies offer incentives or rebates for various green upgrades, such as water-conserving appliances, PV systems, and energy-efficient heating and cooling equipment. Some banks offer special mortgages for energy-efficient homes or homes located in neighborhoods where you don't need a car to get to work, schools, and shops (these are called Location-Efficient Mortgages). These loan programs help borrowers qualify for larger loans on the principle that their energy or transportation costs will be substantially lower than a typical homeowner's.

clean
LIVING:
protecting our air and water

Fresh air and clean water. They're essential to our well-being, yet we tend to take them for granted. We do things every day, often unwittingly, that put the air and water we depend on at risk. As individuals, we can't solve all the environmental problems of the world, but we can pay more attention to what we do at home.

CLEARING THE AIR

We usually associate air pollution with smokestacks and tailpipes, not with the inside of our homes. But the air in our homes can be two to five times more polluted than outdoor air. What causes indoor air pollution? There are obvious sources, such as tobacco smoke or wood smoke from a poorly drafting fireplace. Malfunctioning gas stoves and furnaces can release carbon monoxide into living spaces. In

Above: On this bedroom wall, an eggplant-hued, lime plaster veneer was applied directly on drywall. The plaster is made from natural materials and contains no VOCs. It was sealed with a water-based sealant that's also VOC-free, creating a wall finish that was as healthy to apply as it is to live with.

Opposite: Surfaces such as drapes and wall-to-wall carpet may harbor dust mites, pet dander, mold, and other irritants. With suspicions rising that indoor air contaminants could be linked to increasing asthma rates and other health problems, many people are taking a new look at the furnishings and finishes in their homes. Window coverings that are easy to clean, such as these plantation shutters, and smooth-surface flooring such as wood, concrete, or ceramic tile, may promote better indoor air quality. This home also has a fresh-air ventilation system that draws in outside air and flushes out inside air at regular intervals.

some regions, radon is a concern. Then there are common biological contaminants, including pet dander, mold, and dust mites.

Other sources of indoor pollution are less obvious but may affect our health. Many modern building materials and furnishings—including some types of insulation, plywood, paint, and even upholstery fabrics—are made with chemicals that are released (outgassed) over time into the air we breathe. Depending on the product, these chemicals can include formaldehyde, acetone, chlorinated solvents, phthalates, benzene, and a host of other problematic compounds, many of which are suspected to be carcinogenic or harmful to the central nervous system.

There's so much we don't know about the effects of indoor air pollution on our health. Our bodies are amazingly resilient, and if a home has good ventilation, either through natural or mechanical means, we may never notice any effects from breathing in these pollutants day after day. But for the small number of people who develop severe sensitivities to chemicals commonly found in our homes and workplaces, poor indoor air quality can be debilitating. And there's suspicion that the growing incidence of respiratory illnesses such as asthma, especially among children, could be linked to indoor air pollution.

The most effective way to combat indoor air pollution is to keep out the offending materials in the first place. In many cases, there are healthier substitutes for suspect building components and materials. Fiberglass insulation, for example, once commonly contained formaldehyde, but formaldehyde-free versions are now available.

[The most effective way to combat indoor air pollution is to keep out the offending materials in the first place.]

It's also important that your home have adequate ventilation. Older homes, with their leaky doors and windows and uninsulated walls and ceilings, often had numerous paths through which inside air could flow out and outside air be introduced. Today, because we're building our homes to be more energy efficient and moisture resistant—and because we're bringing into our homes so many more potentially troublesome materials—it sometimes isn't enough to rely on passive ventilation. Some new homes have mechanical ventilation systems that bring outside air into the home at regular intervals, helping to dilute the stale inside air with fresher outside air.

GOOD GREEN RECOMMENDATIONS:
PROTECTING INDOOR AIR QUALITY

Here are a few commonsense steps to protecting air quality in your home.

■ *Adhesives, paints and sealers.* Use solvent-free adhesives and water-based, low- or zero-VOC, formaldehyde-free interior paints and sealers. VOCs pollute the air inside your home (they also contribute to the formation of smog outside). If you've ever noticed that "new paint" smell in a home, you're breathing chemicals offgassing from the paint.

■ *Flooring.* Consider smooth flooring surfaces instead of carpet. Hardwood, concrete, bamboo, and tile floors are easier to keep free of contaminants such as dust mites and pet dander than carpeted surfaces.

■ *Formaldehyde in furnishings and building products.* An array of home furnishings and building products contain formaldehyde, which the U.S. Environmental Protection Agency considers to be a probable human carcinogen. With some products, the formaldehyde will continue to offgas long after you bring the product home. Pressed-wood products such as particleboard, medium density fiberboard, and plywood—often used for furniture, cabinets, countertop substrates and shelves—typically contain a urea-formaldehyde binder. Purchase formaldehyde-free alternatives, solid-wood products, or products with phenol-formaldehyde binders that outgas at a much lower level than urea-formaldehyde binders.

■ *Garages.* Garages that are detached from the home promote better indoor air quality. With attached garages, car exhaust fumes can enter the home through gaps around doors or cracks in the ceilings and walls. If you do have an attached garage, make sure that the door from the garage into your house seals tightly; if it doesn't, install weather stripping to improve the seal. A more expensive solution is to install an exhaust fan in the garage that will automatically run for a while after the garage door has been opened or closed.

■ *Household cleaners.* Use nontoxic household cleaners. If you're using harsh cleaners such as bleach, ammonia-based products, or drain cleaners, read and follow the precautions on the label. If in doubt about the safety of a product, don't use it.

■ *Mold and mildew.* Don't invite mold and mildew into your home. Keep the roof, siding, and windows in good repair so that moisture doesn't get inside roof and wall cavities. Attend to plumbing leaks immediately. If you live in a very humid climate, you may need an air conditioner or a dehumidification system to reduce humidity levels. If you're remodeling or building a new home, make sure your architect and builder pay careful attention to moisture-related design and construction details—you want to prevent as much moisture penetration as possible, and provide avenues for any trapped moisture to escape.

■ *Smoke.* Don't allow smoking in your home. Also, think twice about having a wood-burning fire in your home because of the indoor and outdoor air pollution associated with wood smoke. If you want a fireplace, a sealed-combustion gas fireplace is usually considered a healthier option.

■ *Ventilation fans.* Use your bathroom and kitchen exhaust fans. They draw out stale air, but more importantly they draw out moisture (mold thrives on moisture). Make sure your range hood vents to the outside, particularly if you have a gas stove—you want to get smoke, combustion byproducts, and steam out of your house.

■ *Wallcoverings.* Some wallcoverings, such as vinyl wallpaper, may trap moisture, creating conditions for mold to grow on wallboard. Instead of wallpaper, consider using a zero-VOC paint or a natural plaster finish on your walls.

GREEN-IT-YOURSELF

Scattered across Michiko and Eric Storm's two-acre lot in Northern California are ten apple trees, a remnant of the days when this property was part of the commercial orchard that's still operating next door. Although only a few miles from town, it's a pastoral setting that the couple found well suited to their dream of building a home that would use resources wisely and be delightful and healthy to live in. Although neither had formal building experience, to keep within their tight budget they did most of the design and construction themselves, hiring out the foundation work, much of the framing, the drywall installation, and cabinetmaking.

They spent two years working on the design and researching materials and construction methods, and another two-and-a-half years building while they lived in a trailer on the property. The result: a thoughtfully laid out two-story, 1,400-square-foot home that's comfortable but no bigger than it needs to be. The ground floor includes an open kitchen/dining/living area that's intimately scaled for two people but flexible enough to accommodate large gatherings. Also on the first floor are the master bedroom, a water closet with toilet and sink, and a separate bathing room with a sink, shower, and Japanese-style soaking tub.

The couple designed their home for passive solar heating, with its long axis running east-west and most of the windows in the main living area facing south. Even on the gloomiest days, there's no need to turn the lights on—the interior is

Above: The home takes advantage of the sun's free energy. South-facing windows fill the great room with daylight year-round, while roof eaves keep the hot summer sun off the windows. In the winter, when the sun is at a lower angle, direct beams of sunlight enter the great room, helping to heat the home.

Opposite: With a dazzling wildflower display like this, who needs a lawn?

bathed in daylight. Low-e windows with an argon-gas fill keep warmth inside when the weather's cool. A skylit stairwell brightens the home's core. Upstairs, a guestroom and a workspace nestle under the steeply pitched roof. With its compact design, the actual footprint of the house is a modest 880 square feet. A detached garage provides extra storage space.

The couple employed a number of low-tech strategies that promote good indoor air quality. A bench just inside the front door provides a convenient place for removing and storing shoes to avoid tracking pollutants into the home, and there's no carpet to harbor contaminants. A hydronic radiant-floor heating system provides gentle heat without stirring up dust the way that ducted heating systems do. What's more, they avoided formaldehyde-containing building materials and used low-VOC paints and finishes throughout the interior.

Outside, Eric and Michiko worked with the land to encourage healthy soil and vegetation. Rather than install a 2,500-gallon tank on the property to store water required by the local fire-safety code, they dug a retention pond that's now teaming with frogs and birds, and is ringed with wildflowers. On a section of the property eroded by storm water runoff, they created swales to slow the flow of rainwater and give it time to percolate into the ground. As much work as they put into the land, it gives back—from the organic vegetables harvested from the garden each summer to the bushels of apples the old trees produce each fall.

[**Low-tech strategies can promote good indoor air quality.**]

Above: Smooth-surfaced floors like wood and tile help to maintain good indoor air quality. Low-VOC paints and finishes were used throughout this house, and building products containing formaldehyde were avoided. A detached garage keeps car fumes out of the home.

Opposite: The house is compact but thoughtfully designed for convenience and comfort. A small water closet with toilet and sink (left) are in a separate room from the shower and tub (right). The soaking tub looks onto a serene, secluded garden.

In Tucson, the Civano development has reduced potable water consumption by 65 percent compared to an average Tucson home. Only native plants and plants adapted to the Sonoran desert environment are used for landscaping. During the winter rains and summer monsoons, rainfall is channeled to planted areas or stored in cisterns for later use. In addition, homes have access to Tucson's reclaimed water system for irrigation. In this garden, a sign boasts, "I'm saving groundwater by watering my yard with reclaimed water."

WATER, WATER EVERYWHERE

Seventy percent of the earth's surface is covered with water, yet more than two billion people live in regions where there's not enough clean freshwater to meet agricultural, industrial, and household needs. Access to uncontaminated freshwater may be the most pressing global environmental challenge of coming years.

Reducing water use inside and around our homes is probably the easiest and most effective step we can take to help safeguard our water supplies. Using less water slows the rate at which ground and surface water supplies are depleted. It also reduces stress on our overburdened municipal freshwater and wastewater treatment systems. Water conservation may require small changes in habit, but it's an easy way to make a difference.

GOOD GREEN RECOMMENDATIONS: USING LESS WATER INSIDE

■ *Use water-conserving plumbing fixtures* such as low-flow showerheads and faucet aerators. They don't cost much (especially if your local water company offers rebates), can be bought at home improvement stores, and can cut a fixture's water use by as much as 40 percent without noticeably diminishing performance.

■ *Replace older toilets.* If your toilets were installed before 1994 (when the U.S. government began mandating the installation of low-flow toilets in new home construction), consider replacing them with low-flow models. Check with your municipal water company for rebate offers.

■ *Purchase water-efficient appliances.* If you're in the market for a new dishwasher or washing machine, look for water-conserving models. Check with your local utility or water company for available rebates.

■ *Consider composting toilets if you live in a remote area.* Composting toilets use no water. Instead of being hooked up to a sewer system or septic tank, a composting toilet is connected to a composting chamber. In that chamber, aerobic bacteria breaks down waste, turning it into a soil-like humus that can be used as fertilizer on non-edible plants or can be removed by a licensed hauler, depending on local regulations. Check with your local building department about restrictions that may apply.

GOOD **GREEN** RECOMMENDATIONS:
WATER-SAVVY LANDSCAPING

■ *Plant native or climate-appropriate plants* that don't require excessive irrigation. In very dry climates or places that experience frequent water shortages, use drought-tolerant plants.

■ *Collect graywater for irrigating your yard.* Graywater is the relatively clean wastewater from sinks, showers, and washing machines (not the so-called "blackwater" from toilets). With a typical graywater system, pipes carry the graywater from the house through a filtering medium, and then to a tank where it is stored for later use. To minimize health risks, it's usually used for below-surface irrigation of nonedible plants. Check with local building officials about graywater regulations in your area—some communities restrict its use.

■ *Harvest rainwater for irrigation.* Rainwater harvesting systems typically direct rainwater runoff from the roof through gutters and downspouts to an aboveground or underground cistern, from which the water can then be pumped to irrigate a yard or garden. Some households, especially in remote areas, also collect and purify rainwater for drinking, but this may be subject to local ordinances.

■ *Shrink your lawn.* If you want a grass lawn, consider limiting its size—you'll spend less time mowing the lawn, and you'll use less water too. To reduce the amount of storm water that runs off your property, consider planting more trees and shrubs—they do a better job of absorbing rainwater than turf does.

■ *Go organic.* Organic gardening means gardening in cooperation with nature: relying on environmentally friendly techniques and substances such as compost, mulch, and manure to build healthy soils, manage pests, and encourage plants to flourish. To prevent potentially harmful chemicals from contaminating waterways, eliminate or limit your use of synthetic pesticides and herbicides. One easy way to keep the weeds out of your garden without resorting to herbicides is to use a weed barrier fabric. The fabric allows water, air, and nutrients to pass through while blocking weed growth. It can be cut to fit around your plants and covered with rock or bark mulch.

■ *Reduce storm water runoff from your property.* Rapidly draining storm water can contaminate streams, lakes, and oceans with oil and other pollutants picked up from parking lots and roads. To keep storm water on-site and allow it to percolate into the ground, reduce the amount of impervious paving on your property. Instead of a concrete patio, for example, consider paving blocks, bricks, or flagstones laid in sand (not cemented together). Consider gravel or decomposed granite for walkways.

■ *Grow a green roof.* Also called living roofs or grass roofs, green roofs are specially engineered flat roofs with a layer of soil or other growing medium on top of a waterproof membrane. Green roofs are often planted with native grasses, wildflowers, and other climate-appropriate groundcover. They help slow the flow of storm water off the roof, keep surrounding outside air temperatures cooler, offer some insulating and sound-absorbing qualities, and may even help protect the roof from deterioration. Green-roof systems can be expensive and fairly complex to install, so it may be some time before they catch on in mainstream American homes.

When a property has a high percentage of impervious surfaces like concrete, asphalt, and roofs, storm water quickly runs off the site, which can over-burden municipal wastewater treatment systems. Storm water runoff also picks up pollutants like pesticides and road oil that can contaminate waterways. Pervious surfaces, such as planted areas or these interlocking driveway pavers set in a bed of sand, reduce runoff by allowing rainwater to filter into the ground.

Left and far left: Rain flows from this home's metal roof into a gutter and then down a "rain chain." The rainwater is stored in a 1,500-gallon underground cistern, and pumped up when needed to irrigate the garden.

This house, part of an infill complex of three affordable-rate homes, was designed to use wood efficiently. Walls were framed with 2 x 6 studs spaced 24 inches apart instead of the more common 16-inch spacing, reducing wood use by 19 percent. All the framing and finish lumber was certified to have come from sustainably harvested forests.

build a
BETTER
wall

A good green home doesn't require unconventional construction methods or building materials. A typical wood-framed house—if it's built well with good insulation, a tight building envelope, and high-performance windows—can be as environmentally friendly as a house with all the latest green bells and whistles.

It's easier being green if you don't stray far from familiar building methods and commonplace materials. For one thing, it's simpler to find builders, subcontractors, and suppliers familiar with standard home-building methods such as wood-framing, hanging drywall, and insulating with fiberglass batts than to find tradespeople who know how to ram an earthen wall or build a house with straw bales. It's certainly less complicated to get a building permit if you adhere to conventional methods. If you're remodeling or building a new house and are short on money, time, or both, consider sticking with tried-and-true methods and materials, while tweaking them to achieve a higher environmental performance.

There are, of course, alternatives to conventional wood-framed construction. This chapter provides an overview of a number of construction methods, including more advanced wood-framing strategies, steel framing, building with straw bales, and earth-building techniques.

WOOD FRAMING

Americans like building with wood. At least 90 percent of the 1.2 million single-family houses built in the United States each year are wood-framed (also called "stick-framed"). That's a lot of wood: More than 13,000 board feet of framing lumber alone goes into a 2,000-square-foot house. But it's possible to build a stick-framed house that uses 15 to 30 percent less wood than today's average house without spending more money or sacrificing strength or durability. Here are common ways that it's done:

Trusses—Traditionally, the rafters, ceiling joists, and floor joists of wood-framed homes were built at the construction site. Today it's becoming more common to use prefabricated trusses, which are load-bearing frameworks manufactured at a factory and shipped to the building site. These structural components are fashioned of small pieces of wood joined with metal plates, and can be specified for most home designs. Advantages include faster framing, reduced wood use, and the ability to have longer floor and roof spans.

Engineered wood products—Manufactured from wood fibers bound with adhesives, they use significantly less wood than the solid sawn lumber they replace. They're generally lighter, stronger, and straighter. The wood fiber in engineered wood comes from small-diameter trees, reducing pressure to cut down our remaining old-growth trees. Engineered wood products include glued laminated timber (glulam), parallel strand lumber, wood I-joists, and oriented strand board (OSB). When possible, purchase engineered wood manufactured with formalde-hyde-free adhesives and FSC-certified wood fibers.

Structural insulated panels (SIPs)—As an alternative to framing a home with wood studs, SIPs can be used to build floors, walls, and roofs in new construction and additions. SIPs typically consist of rigid foam insulation sandwiched between two panels of oriented strand board. They're prefabricated and shipped to the construction site ready to install, greatly reducing the labor required to frame a home. Homes built with SIPs can be very energy efficient because the panels provide uniform insulation coverage and reduced air infiltration compared to conventionally insulated wood-framed homes.

Advanced wood-framing—This encompasses a set of building practices that can save money and dramatically reduce wood use without compromising a building's strength. The three-unit housing complex shown on page 110 was built with a variety of advanced framing techniques, including framing walls with twenty-four-inch spacing instead of the more conventional sixteen inches, which reduced wood use by 19 percent. Other advanced framing measures include using a slab-on-grade ground floor instead of a wood-framed floor, framing corners with two studs instead of three, and using box headers instead of standard headers. Box headers are less expen-sive, stronger, and use less wood than standard headers. The wood used for box headers typically comes from smaller, younger trees, whereas the large-dimension lumber for standard headers generally comes from old-growth trees.

HILLSIDE OASIS

When Ian Nabeshima and Henry Kahle decided to rebuild on the site of a home that had burned to the ground, they didn't set out to replicate the beloved Tudor-style cottage they had lost. Instead, they imagined a different kind of home, one that would be modern and original, yet modestly sized and built with a relatively tight budget. They teamed up with Karl Wanaselja, a young architect and builder who brought to the project a passion for combining good design with environmentally smart building methods and materials. The result—very much a collaborative effort between the owners and architect—is a home whose understated elegance is rooted in an ethic of caring about our planet's future.

At 1,600 square feet, this two-bedroom house in Oakland, California, isn't large, but it feels remarkably roomy in part because so much space is "borrowed" from outside. The home's east wall consists almost entirely of oversized industrial-style glass doors, some of which haul up like a garage door, while others roll aside. With the doors open, the living and dining areas and the downstairs bedroom seem to melt into the lush secluded garden. Even with the doors closed, the home feels exuberantly transparent, thanks to this two-story wall of glass.

A twenty-six-foot ceiling in the main living area also helps the home live larger. Along a wall that's washed in light from a curving skylight, an open

Concrete walls and floors serve as both structural elements and finish materials.

Opposite and left: Industrial-style doors can be hauled up, dissolving the distinction between inside and out.

Bottom left: This column was milled from a tree killed by the Oakland firestorm that destroyed the owners' previous home.

staircase climbs to the loft. Hovering above the main living area like a wide catwalk, the loft includes a built-in sitting nook and an open office with views of the living room below and the garden just outside. Floor-to-ceiling bookshelves roll on a barn-door style track to separate the loft from the second-floor bedroom and bath.

The house combines concrete walls on the first floor with wood-framed construction on the second level. Many of the structural elements do double-duty as finish materials, a savvy way to use fewer resources when building a home. The concrete walls are exposed and unpainted, their surfaces embossed with horizontal ridges left by the temporary form boards into which the concrete had been poured. The concrete floor slab has been elegantly stained to serve as the finish floor. These walls and the floor act as thermal batteries, absorbing the sun's heat during the day and releasing it to the interior at night when temperatures cool. During the colder months, the floor stays warm underfoot, thanks to a heated slab (warm water circulates through pipes embedded in the concrete).

The home's design treats wood with care. The large structural beams aren't milled from old-growth trees. Instead, they're glulams and parallel strand lumber—engineered wood products manufactured from tree fibers bound with adhesives. The second-story floor joists are

Right: Located at the end of a curving road that climbs into the hills, the home is cheek by jowl with neighboring houses and a busy freeway. Nonetheless it feels like an oasis, thanks to over-sized glass doors that open onto a secluded patio and verdant garden.

Opposite: After the concrete was poured for the walls on the main level, the wood form boards were removed, then sanded and reused for the ceiling. The exposed beams are engineered lumber products.

Bottom right: Bookshelves mounted on a sliding track separate the upstairs bedroom from the loft. A balcony overlooking the garden extends the bedroom's livable space.

reclaimed cedar bought from a building salvage company.

Other eco-intelligent features include insulation made from recycled newspapers, and a solar collector on the roof that preheats water for household needs. And when it rains, rainwater is channeled to one corner of the metal roof and flows down a rain chain, where it fills a 1,500-gallon cistern that's buried in the ground (see photos on page 109). A pump brings up the rainwater when needed to irrigate the garden.

Remarkably, little about this house overtly calls attention to its eco-friendly features. It is, first and fore-most, a gem of a home that's as delightful to live in as it is to look at.

STEEL FRAMING

Steel framing has been used for years in multifamily residential and commercial buildings, but it's still relatively rare for single-family homes. It's gaining momentum, though, especially in places like Hawaii and the Gulf states where termites and moisture wreak havoc with wood. As a building material, light-gauge steel has a lot going for it. It's durable and fire resistant. Steel framing doesn't rot and insects don't like it. It's strong, dimensionally stable, and manufactured to exacting standards. It's 100-percent recyclable and has a high recycled content.

[Steel framing doesn't rot and insects don't like it.]

In the past, perhaps the biggest drawback to steel framing was its energy performance. Compared to wood, steel is highly conductive, meaning that heat readily transfers through it. Using uninsulated steel for exterior walls provides an easy path for unwanted heat from the outside to be drawn into the home, and for heat from within the home to be drawn out. This process, called *thermal bridging,* results in excess energy being used to cool and heat the home. Thermal bridging can also cause condensation problems, creating conditions for mold growth. A common way to combat thermal bridging is to affix panels of rigid insulation to the exterior of the steel framing. Steel studs are an excellent choice for framing interior walls where thermal bridging isn't a concern.

STRAW BALE HOMES

Living in a straw bale house used to invite the inevitable jokes about huffing and puffing and blowing the house down. That's changing. Recently straw bale building has been undergoing a revival of sorts, having evolved considerably since Nebraska settlers built the first straw bale homes in the late 1800s.

Straw bale houses come in two basic forms. In a load-bearing design, the walls are formed of stacked straw bales that carry some or all of the roof's weight. More common today, however, and more likely to be acceptable to local building officials, is the infill design, in which the bales are stacked within a structural framework (wood, steel, or masonry can be used). Construction details vary, but the bales are often pinned together with reinforcing steel dowels ("rebar"). An exterior finish of stucco is typically applied to wire mesh that's attached to the

Left: A "truth window" proves to skeptics what lies beneath the surface.

Bottom: Straw bales can be used as insulating infill for exterior walls. Here they were also used to create stepped partition walls that flank the entry inside and out. One of the advantages of straw bale construction is the ease with which curved, sculptural walls can be created.

bales. Interior walls are often finished with plaster, or drywall can be used.

People who have built straw bale homes extol their virtues. Straw is an abundant renewable resource—it's the waste that's left over after harvesting rice, wheat, barley, and other grains. Depending on the size of the bale and how it is stacked, the walls are fourteen to twenty-four inches thick. The bales do an impressive job of insulating, making for a quiet comfortable home and reducing heating and cooling bills. Tests of straw bale walls have shown them to be fire and pest resistant. The thick sheltering walls provide a sense of sanctuary and have an emotional resonance that few homes built of mass-produced materials offer.

Straw bale construction isn't the best solution for every house, however. Thick bale walls don't make as much sense on tight urban plots where space is at a premium. Building a straw bale house is labor intensive and there aren't many builders familiar with straw bale construction methods, so it can be more expensive than a conventional wood-framed house.

Moisture is perhaps the biggest concern. If moisture gets trapped in a straw bale wall, mold or rot can take hold. It's critical that the bales be kept dry before, during, and after construction. Straw bale homes can be built in most climates as long as care is taken to protect the walls from moisture by setting them on a good foundation with a moisture-proofed top, providing a roof with generous overhangs, and using breathable wall finishes such as stucco and plaster.

A HOUSE OF STRAW

With its thick straw bale walls that curve like embracing arms and its colorful plaster finishes, this home in the hills above Northern California's Silicon Valley has a contemporary organic feel. At 3,200 square feet, the house, which includes a detached work studio that doubles as a guest suite, isn't small, but it hugs the ground, blending gracefully with the wooded ridge on which it sits. Straw bale infill construction was used for the north, east, and west exposures, while a wood-framed wall with large expanses of glass faces south.

Straw bales are far from the only feature that makes this a good green home. The roof is framed with structural insulated panels (SIPs), a prefabricated assembly of rigid foam insulation sandwiched between two sheets of oriented strand board. The panels fit together snugly, creating an energy-efficient roof structure.

The house is designed for passive solar heating and natural cooling, with its longest exposure facing south. The home remains comfortable in the summer without air conditioning, thanks to good cross-ventilation as well as roof eaves and a patio trellis that shade the south-facing windows. In the winter when the sun is at a lower angle, direct sunbeams enter the interior and strike the dark, acid-washed concrete floors. The concrete's thermal mass stores the sun's heat, releasing it into the home as temperatures drop in the evening. A heated floor slab (a hydronic radiant-floor heating system) provides additional warmth when needed.

The owner, working with Van der Ryn Architects, a renowned ecological design

Left: Curving straw bale walls create an inviting entry. An iron-oxide wash applied to the stucco creates a wonderfully rich, mottled, terra-cotta finish. The door is old-growth fir reclaimed from an abandoned shed that once stood on the property.

Opposite: Instead of painting the interior walls, the drywall was plastered and then finished with a colorful lime wash.

firm, was closely involved in the home's design and helped guide the selection of green features. She and her family and friends even got together for an old-fashioned bale-raising, pitching in to stack the bales within the building's shell. They helped create the curved walls by—believe it or not—delivering hard kicks to the bales to mold them into the desired shapes! The owner's environmental sensibilities extended to the home's interior design. Closet doors are fashioned of storm-felled cedar, light sconces are handcrafted of recycled tin and found objects, and vintage lighting fixtures, sinks, and tubs add old-world charm.

Left: Set back from the ridge and kept low so as not to dominate the land, the house's main living areas face south with a view of wooded hills. On the left, a carport with a straw bale back wall connects a studio/guest room with the main house. The framed portions of the house are clad in fiber-cement exterior siding, while terra-cotta-hued stucco covers the straw bale walls.

Opposite: The east, west, and north walls were built with straw bales, as were the curving, stepped partition walls inside and outside the front entry. Hand-peeled, salvaged cedar columns contribute to the lively play of textures.

Above: This home's south-facing windows allow in plenty of daylight, while exterior overhangs keep direct beams of sun from overheating the house during the summer. High clerestory windows can be opened to vent hot air. In the winter, the cinnamon-colored concrete floor acts as a thermal battery to absorb the sun's heat and slowly release it into the home.

BUILDING WITH EARTH

People have been using earth to build homes for thousands of years. Today, a distinction is often made between heavily processed masonry construction materials, such as fired clay bricks and concrete blocks, and more raw materials such as unfired adobe bricks and rammed earth.

In the United States, fired brick is used today primarily as exterior siding rather than as a load-bearing component. Concrete masonry units or concrete blocks, however, are a fairly common home-building material in some regions, such as the South. To improve energy performance, concrete block products have been developed that combine concrete with plastic foam insulation. Another innovative product is autoclaved aerated concrete, which is used to create a solid but lightweight concrete block that provides better insulation than standard blocks.

Insulated concrete forms (ICFs) have also been gaining popularity, thanks to their energy-efficient advantages. With standard poured-in-place concrete construction, wood formwork is erected, concrete is poured into the forms, and the forms are pulled away after the concrete walls harden. ICFs use foam forms instead of wood, and the foam remains in place permanently after the concrete cures. The foam insulates the walls, creating a comfortable and quiet home (standard finishes are attached to the walls, including interior drywall and exterior siding).

Of the more raw earth-building methods, adobe and rammed earth are probably the most common and are discussed in the following sections. Besides adobe and rammed earth, there's an array of other earth-based building techniques, including cob, light straw-clay, earthbag, and pumicecrete, but most of these methods don't meet building code requirements and are for now considered experimental.

ADOBE

Adobe bricks are made with a mix of clay, sand, and water that's poured or pressed into forms and air dried. These unfired bricks may have additives such as asphalt emulsion to retard moisture or cement to stabilize the soil. While occasionally made at the building site, in the United States today adobe bricks are more likely to be purchased from a commercial distributor.

After drying, the unfired bricks are mortared together on top of a foundation to create walls. Adobe walls are customarily finished with stucco or plaster, although in climates with little rain

Above: An adobe wall shelters a private garden alongside this rammed-earth house. Downtown Tucson's high-rises are close by, yet this residential neighborhood feels like a place apart.

Left: In very dry climates, the exterior of adobe walls can be left exposed. The fluted metal spouts, called canales, *drain rainwater from the roof and keep it off the walls.*

it's possible to leave the adobe bare. A roof with wide over-hangs will help protect exposed adobe walls from erosion.

Unlike straw bale, adobe has a very low R-value, so additional insulation—usually plastic foam applied to the exterior—is needed in many climates. Although a poor insulator, adobe walls—typically sixteen-inches thick—provide outstanding thermal mass, making them a good green option for regions such as the American Southwest, where adobe is a time-honored building method.

RAMMED AND SPRAYED EARTH

Rammed and sprayed earth-building techniques create monolithic walls with a unique look that manages to feel both contemporary and timeless. To create a rammed-earth wall, a mix of clay, sand, water, and often cement is placed into temporary forms much like those used for pouring concrete walls. The mixture is rammed into the forms in six- to eight-inch layers called "lifts" until compressed to a rock-like hardness. Another lift is added and rammed, and the process is repeated until the top of the form is reached.

The ramming process results in straight distinctive walls—often twelve to eighteen inches thick—that can be left exposed inside and out or finished with plaster. Varying the soil mixtures in the lifts can create lovely striations of subtle color. Surface cracks may develop that add character, but the walls are fully structural, don't shrink, and hold up well to freeze-and-thaw cycles. Rammed earth provides excellent thermal mass, but isn't a good insulator, so in cold climates insulation such as rigid foam panels may be attached to the outside walls and finished with stucco.

Sprayed earth is a variation of rammed earth developed by David Easton, one of the pioneers of modern earth building in the United States. This method, which he calls "PISE" for pneumatically installed stabilized earth, entails using a high-pressure hose to shoot a wet soil mix against open formwork, building up thick walls quickly. Excess soil is scraped from the form using a taut wire. Spraying the earth instead of ramming it speeds up the process considerably, saving time and money.

Because of the labor involved, rammed- and sprayed-earth construction is unlikely to be adopted by builders who erect hundreds or thousands of houses a year. But for custom builders working in regions where it makes sense to build homes with high thermal mass, rammed and sprayed earth can be used to create homes of unparalleled resilience and beauty.

Above and opposite: Rammed-earth walls are attractive and durable enough to be left exposed inside and out.

Right: In this rammed-earth home that's under construction, an interior courtyard has whimsical candle niches carved into the earthen wall.

WINE COUNTRY RETREAT

It's been said that the environmental movement is lacking an aesthetic, and that green buildings, for all their good intentions, are frumpy or peculiar or downright ugly. In a few cases that may be true, but graceless houses can be found everywhere, regardless of the extent to which sustainability figures into their design.

But green design *can* be good design, as this home in the wine country north of San Francisco so strikingly illustrates. It's a modern house that's rooted in a thoughtful and caring approach to the land and natural resources.

The owners, John Caner and George Beier, wanted a weekend retreat suited to the undulating hills and expansive vistas their twenty-acre property offered—a home that would be built with environmentally sustainable materials but that wouldn't compromise beauty. Of the dozen architects they interviewed, many recommended perching the house on an exposed knoll from which it would command majestic views—and from which it could be seen for miles around. But when architects David Arkin and Anni Tilt saw the property, with its hills of craggy oak and madrone trees and waving grasses, they had a different vision. Nestle the house into a saddle between the hills, they suggested, and break up the dwelling into three separate structures, each of which could be "tuned" to best take advantage of views and light.

Although the three buildings have distinctive characters, the 2,680-square-foot home feels cohesive, thanks to the clay-colored sprayed-earth construction used for the home's major walls. A tower with a guest suite occupying its base has stairs of metal and reclaimed wood that wrap around the exterior of the earthen walls. An office on the second-floor is capped by a small third-floor deck ideal for savoring views of rolling hills, vineyards, and the distant San Francisco Bay.

The earthen walls' thick mass makes them well suited to this particular climate, where for much of the year hot

Opposite: The tower is built with a lively mix of materials: plywood and batten siding at the base, sprayed-earth tower walls, corrugated metal roofing, and railings of reclaimed wood.

Above: Climbing vines readily cling to the rough exterior of a sprayed-earth wall.

The dramatic interplay of natural and constructed elements—earthen walls, seductive pools of water, wide-open skies punctuated by a tower—defines this house in Northern California's wine country. While little about this home shouts "green," a thoughtful, environmentally aware approach informed the entire project.

sunny days give way to significantly cooler nights. While the exterior of the sprayed-earth walls has a rough nubby texture, the interior—where the damp earth mixture was shot against plywood panels—is exceptionally smooth. To fill in some of the pockmarks and fine cracks that remained after the plywood was removed, a thin grout wash was sponged over the interior walls.

A second building contains the great room, kitchen, and breakfast nook. The kitchen has a casual feel, with concrete counters colored a cheery yellow, and casement windows that can be thrown open to scoop in breezes. A counter topped with wood from an old bowling lane separates the more intimate kitchen from the great room's lofty space. At the south end of the great room, large windows high on the wall suffuse the space with daylight, while the room's north end nudges into the hillside. French doors along the western wall open onto a loggia that provides expansive views while sheltering the building from the scorching afternoon sun. A fireplace of rammed earth—the great room's focal point—has striations reminiscent of a canyon wall's layers of sedimentary deposits.

Two bedrooms and another small office occupy the third

The clay-colored, sprayed-earth wall and azure tiles echo the golden hills and blue sky visible through the window.

Above: A lower ceiling in the kitchen creates a more intimate space in contrast with the great room's high ceiling. Casement windows swing wide open to scoop in cooling breezes.

Left: The home sits in a sheltering saddle rather than on a knoll where it would dominate the landscape.

Right: Jewel-like fragments of polished recycled glass enliven this counter.

Below: The home has no air conditioning despite sizzling summer days. All three buildings take advantage of natural cooling, with windows positioned to encourage cross-breezes. Earthen walls and concrete floors provide thermal mass to moderate interior temperatures.

Above: The rammed-earth fireplace and 18-inch-thick, sprayed-earth walls are made from a mix of local quarry waste, cement, and sand. Ceiling trusses are reclaimed Douglas fir, while the cypress for the ceiling decking was salvaged from pickle barrel staves. High south-facing windows at the gabled end of the room admit direct sun in the winter to help warm the house, while roof overhangs keep out the hot summer sun.

Left: Rammed-earth columns support the roof of the loggia, which keeps sun off the western wall.

building, a one-room-deep rectangle that parallels a 75 x 8-foot lap pool. The three buildings are united by a sheltered patio with areas for outdoor cooking, relaxing under a grapevine arbor, or sunning by the pool. It's a unique home where indoor and outdoor spaces effortlessly intertwine, and the soothing tones of clay and old wood create a subtly rustic and utterly alluring retreat.

use the RIGHT stuff

Since the start of the Industrial Revolution we've adopted a brute-force approach to the earth's bounty: take as much as we can, as fast as we can, as cheaply as we can. This path has brought extraordinary wealth to some people. It has provided hundreds of millions of others with products that are inexpensive and convenient, that improve life and health, that bring delight. It has also wrought havoc across the globe, degrading habitats, triggering the extinction of species, and causing social upheaval.

There are signs that our society is shifting to a new industrial paradigm that's more regenerative and less destructive. Many successful companies these days strive to use less energy and fewer resources and to reduce waste and pollution—not necessarily because it's the right thing to do, but because it's the profitable thing to do. Some forward-looking companies are exploring ways to make products and deliver services that give back more than they take.

Some factories now return cleaner water to our rivers than they took out. Some forestry companies treat the land as if their business is going to depend on it forever. Some consumer products companies have begun taking back their goods when the consumer is done with them, and recycling or remanufacturing the materials into new products so that there's no waste.

But we can't leave it up to businesses to lead us to a sustainable future. It's largely consumer demand that drives industry to pull resources out of the ground in the first place. Whether a product is made from a raw material that's renewable or nonrenewable, there's an environmental consequence to extracting, harvesting, processing, installing, using, and ultimately getting rid of the stuff.

Right: The thick walls of a straw bale home encourage sculptural touches, like this deep window reveal. The bales provide excellent insulation and put agricultural waste to good use.

Opposite: The floor panels in this bedroom are made of sunflower-seed hulls—an agricultural waste product.

There are no perfect paths—
everything we buy or use has
consequences.

There are no perfect paths—*everything* we buy or use has consequences for the environment. Still, you can make choices about what you put inside your home—from the floor under your feet to the paint on your walls—that will contribute to a healthier home and a more sustainable future.

HEALTHY HOME, HEALTHY PLANET

When choosing products and materials to use in your home, remember that some products contain components that are potentially hazardous to human health. For example, bookshelves made with particleboard may cost less than shelves of solid sawn lumber, but that particleboard could contain urea-formaldehyde binders that will offgas into your home.

The subject of healthy home furnishings and building materials is complex, and there are dozens of books and Websites with detailed information that can help you make healthier product selections. Here are just a few questions to ask yourself (or the retailer or product manufacturer) when you're selecting a new material or product to use in your home:

Is it safe and healthy to use in my home?
Will it introduce irritants or offgas potentially harmful chemicals?
Will I need to use harsh chemicals to clean or maintain it?
Is the harvesting or manufacturing process safe and healthy for workers?
Is there a safe way to reuse, recycle, or dispose of it when I'm done with it?

If you have concerns about a product's safety, try to find an alternative that you'd be more comfortable with.

ONCE IS NOT ENOUGH

Recycling means taking something that's considered waste, changing its form, and making something new. It typically requires considerable industrial processing, with inputs of everything from energy to clean water to virgin materials. Recycling is rarely an environmentally benign loop in which a material is endlessly reprocessed and reused. Instead, many recyclable

Left: Recycled carpet looks, feels, and performs as well as conventional synthetic-fiber carpet, plus it keeps plastic trash out of landfills. About forty two-liter plastic bottles go into a square yard of recycled polyester carpet.

Below: An artist fashioned these lampshades from old vinegar bottles.

materials are actually *downcycled*—they're recycled only one time and then become unrecyclable. A plastic water bottle, for example, can be recycled into polyester used to make a fleece jacket (conventional fleece is made from crude oil). But since the recycled fleece fabric is not *recyclable,* the jacket will be tossed when it's no longer wearable.

Still, recycling and buying products with recycled content are important components of the good green home toolkit. When buying products with recycled content, always look for the highest *post-consumer* content available, because that's what keeps trash out of our landfills and incinerators. (*Post-consumer* recycled content is material that would end up in a landfill or incinerator if it weren't recycled. It's different from *post-industrial* recycled content, which is manufacturing scrap that companies routinely reuse in their production processes.)

Many recycled-content building materials and products are available today. These include carpet, drywall, and plastic lumber for decking and outdoor furniture, fiberglass and cellulose insulation, paint, roofing materials, structural steel framing, and glass tiles.

[Recycling and buying products with recycled content are important components of the good green home toolkit.]

THINK GLOBALLY, BUY LOCALLY

When you use a product that's harvested or made locally, you're helping to sustain your community's economy. Also, less energy is used when materials only need to be transported a short distance instead of across the country or around the world. It's not always possible to find a locally made version of the product you need. But if you look around, you might be surprised by the variety, quality, and beauty of household products and building materials made in your own backyard.

MAKE IT LAST

A material that doesn't need to be replaced, painted, or repaired every few years may save time, money, and resources over the long haul. Some long-lasting materials and products may cost more upfront, but over time, less durable alternatives may wind up costing you more after you factor in maintenance and replacement costs.

When considering different building materials, think about what will hold up better in your climate. If moisture and termites are a problem, for example, steel studs might be a better long-term solution than wood framing for your home. Wood window frames require periodic painting to protect them from moisture, while fiberglass frames don't require any maintenance. For decks, outdoor furniture, and other outdoor uses, recycled plastic lumber, which never needs painting or staining, is an increasingly popular, low-maintenance alternative to wood.

CERTIFIED WOOD: ENCOURAGING RESPONSIBLE FOREST MANAGEMENT

We've heard about the consequences of indiscriminate logging: loss of tropical rainforests and ancient temperate forests; landslides, stream sedimentation, the destruction of fish habitat; displacement of indigenous people and threats to their livelihood.

How can you be certain the hardwood flooring you selected isn't contributing to these problems, or that the beautiful cedar deck you're planning to build won't play a role in the loss of bald eagle habitat in British Columbia?

Here's how: Use FSC-certified wood. The Forest Stewardship Council promotes an international labeling scheme for wood and wood-based products. Wood bearing the FSC logo comes from forests managed by companies that meet FSC's environmental, social, and economic performance standards, including supporting biodiversity, protecting water quality, and respecting the rights of indigenous people.

Other labeling schemes exist, but the FSC's is perhaps the most widely recognized. FSC's chain-of-custody certification process tracks wood from the forest to the retailer's shelves, giving buyers confidence that their purchases are helping to maintain healthy forests. FSC-certified products include framing lumber, siding, shingles, decking, flooring, cabinets, molding, and much more.

RAPIDLY RENEWABLE RESOURCES

Many products in our homes are made from raw materials that are essentially nonrenewable. Virtually any material mined or extracted from the earth—oil, coal, marble, bauxite, titanium—is created at such an extraordinarily slow rate that it is essentially unreplenishable. Some nonrenewable resources are still so seemingly abundant—clay and sand, for example—that there's little fear of running out. Other nonrenewable resources are being consumed at such a rapid rate—oil is one of the most prominent examples—that global peace and the well-being of future generations may depend on finding ways to curb our consumption.

Renewable resources, however, can be harvested repeatedly because they renew

An elegant, durable alternative to hardwood flooring, bamboo is a fast-growing grass that can be harvested in three to five years. Tongue-and-groove bamboo floor planking with a horizontal grain or vertical grain (shown here) is cost competitive with mid-priced hardwoods like oak.

Above left: Warm and quiet underfoot, cork is an attractive alternative to vinyl flooring. (Vinyl flooring is made from polyvinyl chloride, also known as PVC. Some environmental groups have called for a phaseout of PVC because of concerns about potential environmental problems during its manufacture or disposal.) Cork is harvested from the outer bark of cork oak trees, which regenerate their bark and can be reharvested in about ten years.

Above right: This horizontal-grain bamboo floor is durable and attractive. The kitchen countertops are manufactured from a blend of soybeans and wastepaper.

themselves in a relatively short time frame. Trees re-seed themselves, and rainwater seeps through the ground to replenish aquifers. The problem is that we're consuming some renewable resources at a much faster rate than they can be replenished, or we're harvesting them in ways that degrade their ecosystems.

There's a third type of raw material that's increasingly turning up in good green homes: *rapidly renewable* resources. These are primarily agricultural products grown, harvested, and replanted on a relatively short rotation compared to trees. They include bamboo and other grasses, cork, soy, wheat, hemp, cotton, and sisal. Using products made from these fast-growing renewable resources eases the demand for the slower growing, more environmentally sensitive resources.

MATERIALS WITH A PAST

Call it what you will—salvaged, vintage, reclaimed, used, antique—using an item that's been around the block a few times is often a smarter use of resources than buying a new product. Chances are you're already doing this to some degree. An antique clock, a table inherited from a grandparent—we cherish beautiful well-made objects and keep them in circulation for generations.

It isn't only decorative items and furnishings that can be reused. Today, reclaimed building products are big business, with homeowners, architects, and builders clamoring for a piece of the past, paying good money for old boards, windows, beams, tiles, and countless other used

> Using an item that's been around the block a few times is often a smarter use of resources.

materials. No matter what's motivating the demand—whether it's the sheer romance of owning a piece of history or the desire for quality materials and workmanship—putting old stuff to new use is good for our spirits and good for the planet.

In this rammed-earth home under construction, beams and boards reclaimed from an old barn provide character that's hard to achieve with new wood.

MINING THE URBAN FOREST

The quality of reclaimed old-growth lumber and the craftsmanship of vintage fixtures often exceed what's available in today's new products. Reusing old stuff for a remodeling or home-building project, however, requires considerable enthusiasm and perseverance. Unless you're an inveterate do-it-yourselfer, remember that the time and effort it will take you or your builder to prepare and install salvaged materials may outweigh any initial cost savings. But as the following two homes show, in the right hands reclaimed building materials lend themselves to creating homes of considerable distinction and beauty.

A Handcrafted Home

Located off a twisting canyon road above Santa Monica, California, Grant and Cheri Brosius's cottage is nudged into a wooded slope, its entrance almost hidden by a trellis that shades a flagstone patio. A woodworker and contractor who does fine carpentry for clients throughout the Los Angeles area, Grant has transformed the couple's home into a testament to the aesthetic possibilities of reclaimed wood and found materials. Built in 1925 as a vacation getaway, the cabin had undergone piecemeal expansions and renovations over the decades. By 1994, when Grant bought the cabin, it was rundown and inhabited by squatters.

The original one-room building now encompasses about 900 square feet. On the main level there's an open kitchen/dining/living area, a newly added sitting room, and a full bathroom. Downstairs is a bedroom and a combined work space and laundry area. Although the house is small, its open layout and many windows,

Above: The front door is built of termite-damaged wood pulled out of an apartment building after an earthquake. The geometric floor lamp was inspired by a Frank Lloyd Wright design.

Opposite: Concrete floors and plastered walls and ceilings provide a warm backdrop for furnishings and finishes crafted from salvaged wood and found materials. The dining table was made with a panel of curly birch veneer taken from a discarded bed frame. Some of the wood used to build the chairs was salvaged from packing crates. Windows were fashioned from reclaimed Douglas fir.

clerestories, and skylights provide views and plenty of light, making it feel much larger.

A look inside reveals the possibilities of wood culled from various local sources. A gleaming dining table of curly birch veneer led a previous life as a panel providing support underneath someone's mattress. Sleekly modern chairs were made in part from Brazilian wood salvaged from old packing crates. Rustic double doors are genuinely distressed: they're made from termite-damaged boards torn out of an apartment building, streaked black from rain driven by the wind through nail holes. If these doors could sing, they'd sing the blues. Posts and beams were removed from a nearby brick church badly damaged by the Northridge earthquake that struck the Los Angeles area in 1994. Throughout this gem of a house, there's old wood—some of it refined, some if it quite rough—that's been reworked by a craftsman who seems to see through each piece to its promise as a work of art.

Above: A narrow band of interior windows topped by a skylight allows the adjacent bathroom to share daylight with the sitting room. Douglas fir beams came from an earthquake-damaged church.

Opposite: Posts, beams, windows, and doors are fashioned from reclaimed wood. The chair is made from the root of an avocado tree that had fallen in Beverly Hills.

Left: A shaded patio with furniture handcrafted from salvaged wood serves as a gateway to this home, whose unassuming façade cloaks a jewel-like interior.

A New Home For Old Wood

While the warmth and character of reclaimed wood can enhance a remodeled cabin, it's equally at home in a new dwelling, as this house in East Vancouver, British Columbia, illustrates. Before deciding to build a house from the ground up, Sandy Macdonald and Jenny Ma had searched the area for an existing home that would meet their needs. They wanted a reasonably sized house that also contained a separate area for Jenny's work—she practices traditional Chinese medicine. Eventually, they found a small house in a pleasant residential neighborhood of modest postwar houses. The location was right but the house was undistinguished, so they decided to tear it down and rebuild rather than attempt a top-to-bottom remodel.

Sandy, who acted as general contractor although he'd never built a house before, chose local architect Dan Parke, a childhood friend, to design the home. The result is a 1,900-square-foot house, with a detached garage accessible from a back alley. The house is tall—essentially two-and-a-half stories, the maximum allowed by local zoning—to take advantage of spectacular downtown and mountain views visible over neighboring rooftops.

The first floor accommodates a front entry, a guest room and full bath, and a private area with a back entrance for Jenny's examination room, waiting room, and half-bath. The second floor holds open kitchen, dining, and living

Above: Powder-coated steel connects hefty posts and beams of reclaimed wood.

Opposite: A daylight-filled stairwell occupies the southeast corner. The main living spaces face north to capture views of Vancouver's high rises and mountains.

Left: Board-and-batten siding was made with cedar logs salvaged from a construction site that was being cleared.

Right: An open-plan main floor includes kitchen, dining and living areas, with large timbers of reclaimed Douglas fir helping to define each space. Salvaged lumber was used for virtually all the exposed wood.

Opposite: Tall corner windows and stairs with open risers allow southern light into the home. The stairs are built of reclaimed Douglas fir joined with powder-coated steel angles that add a dash of color. Stairwell windows are lightly sandblasted for privacy.

areas. Up one more flight is the master bedroom and bath tucked under the curving roof to stay within zoning height limits. The house is wood-framed, with large exposed posts and beams that add drama and define the spaces within the open-plan main floor.

Uncomfortable with the idea of using old-growth trees for the large timbers, Sandy decided to see if he could find reclaimed lumber. He knew the house was off to a great start when he came across a sale of massive Douglas fir beams that measured 13 x 29 inches and 21-feet long. They came from an old warehouse that was being razed (it had once been part of a large sawmill operation on the nearby Fraser River). Sandy purchased the beams and shipped them to a micro-sawmill, where they were milled into usable sizes.

The superior quality of the reclaimed wood more than compensated for the challenges of transporting, milling, and storing it. The wood was tight-grained with few flaws, setting the tone for the home's clean modern design. In addition to the large posts and beams, much of the wood used in the house is reclaimed lumber, including the stairs, the floor planks, the roof and floor joists, and much of the millwork.

Outside, small areas of board-and-batten cedar siding complement a stucco exterior. The cedar came from a construction site that was being cleared—Sandy hauled away the logs and had them milled to the size he needed. The beautiful curving roof of standing-seam copper was more expensive than a standard metal roof, but Sandy expects it to last for generations with virtually no maintenance. He had such a positive experience hunting down reclaimed wood and building his own home that he has since started his own business: he's now a builder and remodeler with unique expertise in putting old wood to good use.

restoring our WORLD, one home at a time'

As personal and private as our homes may seem, on a fundamental level we all share the same home. We all live downstream from one another. Retreating to less populated areas or building bigger walls around our yards or our neighborhoods are only short-term solutions.

We can start making changes now in our own homes that will put us on the road to a healthier and more environmentally sustainable future. Even small steps—replacing incandescent light bulbs with energy-efficient compact fluorescent lights, improving our homes' insulation, introducing fewer harsh chemicals into our living spaces—can make a difference if we all take part and if we think about each change not as an end in itself but as a step along the path to creating a better future.

> We can start making changes now in our own homes.

We have a choice about the kind of legacy we'll leave. In the future, we may be vilified as the ones who grabbed the best of the planet's resources, or we may be honored as the ones who worked to create prosperity and good health for all. The legacy won't come entirely from the choices we make about our homes, but it's a good place to start.

GLOSSARY

ACID RAIN
Rain that contains a high concentration of acids formed by the mixing of various pollutants—primarily sulfur dioxide and nitrogen oxides—in the atmosphere. It is harmful to plants and aquatic life.

ADAPTABLE BUILDING
A building that can be readily remodeled or reconfigured to meet an occupant's or community's evolving needs.

ADOBE
Unfired, sun-dried bricks made of earth, often stabilized with asphalt additives or cement; a building made of such bricks.

ADVANCED WOOD FRAMING
Design and construction techniques that significantly reduce the amount of wood used to frame a building. Includes strategies such as studs placed 24 inches on center rather than the standard 16 inches on center; two-stud corners; engineered wood products; and roof or floor trusses.

ALTERNATING CURRENT (AC)
Electric current that reverses its direction of flow at regular intervals. In most countries, the electricity provided by utilities is AC electricity.

AUTOCLAVED AERATED CONCRETE (AAC) BLOCK
A solid concrete block that insulates better and weighs much less than standard concrete block. Used for building construction in many parts of the world, but relatively uncommon in the United States.

BAMBOO FLOORING
Flooring made from bamboo, a giant, fast-growing grass with a hollow stem. Bamboo is considered an environmentally friendly alternative to hardwood because it can be harvested every three to five years. Tongue-and-groove bamboo floor planks with a vertical or horizontal grain are available prefinished or unfinished.

BIODIVERSITY
A contraction of "biological" and "diversity." A wide range of living things in a particular region.

BLACKWATER
Wastewater that contains sewage.

BORROWED SPACE
Views and daylight from a nearby space used to enliven and seemingly enlarge a room.

BUILDING ENVELOPE
A building's shell, including exterior walls, windows, doors, roof, and bottom floor.

CELLULOSE INSULATION
Insulation made from wood fiber, primarily recycled newspaper, treated with nontoxic chemicals to retard fire, mold, and insects. Loose-fill cellulose can be blown into attic spaces or packed into wall cavities. Damp-spray cellulose is a damp mix of cellulose and adhesives that is sprayed into wall cavities before hanging drywall.

CERTIFIED WOOD
Wood certified by an independent, third-party certification program to have been grown and harvested using environmentally responsible forestry practices.

CISTERN
A tank, often underground, used to collect and store rainwater for later use.

CLERESTORY
A window or row of windows placed high on a wall, often above the main roof line, used for introducing daylight into a room.

COB CONSTRUCTION
Earth, sand, straw, and water mixed into a thick mud and formed into loaves (cobs) that are stacked to build a thick wall.

COMPACT FLUORESCENT LIGHTBULB (CFL)
A fluorescent lightbulb designed to replace regular incandescent bulbs. It is three to four times more energy-efficient and lasts eight to ten times longer than an incandescent bulb.

CONDITIONED SPACE
An enclosed space supplied with conditioned air from a heating system, a cooling system, or both.

CONDUCTION (THERMAL)
The transfer of heat directly through a material.

COOL ROOF
A roofing material that is very reflective (usually white or very light in color) and has a high emissivity (releases heat very readily). In hot climates, these characteristics keep the roof surface temperature lower and reduce the amount of energy needed to air condition a building.

CORK FLOORING
Flooring, often sold as tiles, made from cork, which is harvested from the outer bark of cork oak trees without having to fell the trees. Cork oaks regenerate their bark and can be reharvested in about ten years.

COTTON INSULATION
Insulation made from recycled cotton-textile trimmings. Typically treated with a nontoxic fire retardant and sold as batts that fit between framing studs.

DAYLIGHTING
The controlled use of natural light (as opposed to electric light) to illuminate a space. The goal is typically to create a stimulating, appealing environment while reducing energy use from electric lighting.

DECONSTRUCTION
Disassembling rather than demolishing a building so that its components can be reused.

DEMAND WATER HEATER
A water heater that saves energy by heating water as it is needed rather than storing hot water in a tank. Also known as an instantaneous or tankless water heater.

DIRECT CURRENT (DC)
Electric current that flows in one direction. Photovoltaic systems convert sunlight into DC electricity. An inverter is then used to convert the DC electricity to alternating current (AC) electricity so that it can be used to power standard household equipment and appliances.

DOUBLE-GLAZED WINDOW
A window with two panes of glass separated by an air space. Compared to single-glazed windows, double-glazed windows significantly reduce heat and sound transmission. Some double-glazed windows contain a gas such as argon or krypton in the air gap to provide additional insulation.

DOWNCYCLING
The process of recycling a relatively high-quality material into a lower-quality material. Downcycling often involves mixing additives with the recycled content to improve its performance. Rather than being infinitely recyclable, these downcycled, hybrid materials often have to be landfilled or incinerated at the end of their useful lives.

EARTHBAG CONSTRUCTION
Buildings, retaining walls, or other structures constructed of sandbags filled with tamped earth.

EMISSIVITY
The capacity of a surface to radiate energy.

ENERGY EFFICIENCY
Using less electricity or fuel than a conventional technology to perform the same task.

ENERGY STAR
A program sponsored jointly by the U.S. Environmental Protection Agency and the U.S. Department of Energy that promotes energy-efficient products, homes, and technologies for

consumers and businesses. Energy Star–qualified products and new homes are often 10 to 30 percent more efficient than their conventional counterparts.

ENERGYGUIDE LABEL
A yellow sticker required by U.S. law on certain new household appliances, including air conditioners, furnaces, clothes washers, dishwashers, refrigerators, and freezers. The label provides information on the amount of energy the appliance will use in one year.

ENGINEERED WOOD
Building products, including beams, framing studs, and floor and roof joists, made from wood fibers bound with adhesives. The wood typically comes from plantation-grown trees, thus reducing demand for old-growth trees. In general, engineered wood products result in less wood waste than solid-sawn lumber products.

FIBER-CEMENT SIDING
An exterior siding product made from a blend of portland cement, sand, cellulose fiber, and additives. It's typically sold as planks or panels, with a smooth or textured finish.

FLY ASH
A waste product from coal-fired electric power plants that can be used as a substitute for portland cement in some concrete mixtures.

FOOTPRINT
The area of land covered by a building.

FOREST STEWARDSHIP COUNCIL (FSC)
An international certification organization that has established voluntary environmental forest-management standards. FSC accredits independent third-party organizations that monitor and certify the compliance of forestry operations with FSC standards. FSC-labeled wood products give consumers assurance that the wood comes from trees grown and harvested in an environmentally responsible manner.

FORMALDEHYDE
A colorless, pungent gas used in many glues, adhesives, preservatives, and coatings. It also occurs naturally. Products and materials containing formaldehyde can offgas the chemical into the air. According to the U.S. Environmental Protection Agency, exposure to formaldehyde may cause allergic reactions, respiratory problems, or cancer in humans.

FOSSIL FUEL
A fuel such as natural gas, oil, or coal, formed from the decomposition of animals and plants millions of years ago.

FSC
See Forest Stewardship Council.

GLAZING
Transparent or translucent material such as glass or plastic that lets light into a building.

GLOBAL WARMING
The long-term warming of the planet caused by heat trapped in the lower atmosphere by greenhouse gases. These gases are emitted primarily as a result of human activities, including burning fossil fuels.

GLULAM
Abbreviation of "glued laminated" timber. An engineered wood product consisting of thin layers of wood, usually less than two inches thick, bound with an adhesive and formed into structural beams that can be used instead of solid-sawn lumber.

GRAYWATER
Household wastewater that doesn't contain sewage and can be reused for irrigation. Graywater typically comes from showers, dishwashers, and clothes-washing machines.

GREEN BUILDING
Building practices that use energy, water, and other resources wisely so that present and future generations can live well without needlessly damaging the environment.

GREEN ROOF
A roof that has a layer of soil or other growing medium on top of a waterproofing membrane. May be planted with sedum, grasses, wildflowers, or other groundcover. Also known as a "living roof" or "eco roof."

GREENHOUSE GAS
Gases that trap heat in the atmosphere, contributing to global warming. Greenhouse gases, which are primarily the result of human activities such as burning fossil fuels, include carbon dioxide, methane, nitrous oxide, and hydrofluorocarbons.

GREENWASHING
Falsely claiming that a product, service, or company is environmentally responsible.

HABITAT
The region where an animal or plant naturally lives.

HALOGEN LIGHTBULB
A type of incandescent lightbulb that is filled with halogen gas. It burns longer than a standard incandescent bulb and provides a crisp white light, but gets very hot and is less energy efficient than a compact fluorescent bulb.

HEAT EXCHANGER
An energy-saving device that takes waste heat from one process and reuses it in another process. For

example, an air-to-air heat exchanger (also known as a heat-recovery ventilator) captures heat from indoor air that's about to be vented from a home and transfers that heat to fresh air that's being drawn in from the outside.

HEAT GAIN
Heat from the sun, people, electric lights, or appliances that causes the temperature in a space to rise.

HEAT ISLAND EFFECT
The tendency of large areas of roofs, asphalt, concrete, and paved surfaces to absorb the sun's heat, making urban areas considerably hotter than nearby rural areas.

HEAT LOSS
The decrease of heat in a space as a result of heat escaping through the building's walls, windows, roof, and other building envelope components.

HIGH PERFORMANCE
A building or building component designed to be more energy or resource efficient, healthy, and comfortable than a conventional building or building component.

HORIZONTAL-AXIS WASHING MACHINE
A clothes washer with a horizontal tub instead of a vertical tub (most horizontal-axis washers have doors in the front of the machine rather than on top). Horizontal-axis washers tend to use significantly less water—and therefore less energy to heat the water—than conventional washers.

HYDRONIC RADIANT-FLOOR HEATING SYSTEM
A heating system in which warm water circulates through tubes embedded in a concrete floor slab or attached beneath the subflooring. The floor absorbs heat from the tubes and slowly releases it to the room, providing a comfortable, quiet, gentle warmth that doesn't stir up dust or create drafts.

IMPERVIOUS SURFACE
A surface that water can't pass through.

INCANDESCENT LIGHTBULB
A lightbulb that consists of a filament inside a glass bulb. Passing electric current through the filament causes it to heat up and produce light. Standard household lightbulbs are incandescent bulbs; they are very inefficient because up to 90 percent of the energy they consume results in wasted heat instead of useful light.

INDOOR AIR QUALITY
The nature of air inside a building. Indoor air-pollution sources include tobacco and wood smoke; certain

building materials and furnishings; certain cleaning, maintenance, and personal care products; dust mites; pet dander; mold; radon; pesticides; and outdoor air pollution. Inadequate ventilation and high humidity levels can also contribute to indoor air-quality problems.

INFILL DEVELOPMENT
Building on empty or underutilized lots in cities or older suburban areas instead of building in a previously undeveloped area.

INFILTRATION
The movement of outdoor air into a building through cracks and other defects around doors, windows, walls, roofs, and floors.

INSTANTANEOUS WATER HEATER
See demand water heater.

INSULATED CONCRETE FORM (ICF)
Plastic foam shaped into hollow blocks, panels, or planks and used as a form to create a concrete wall. After positioning the foam forms, rebar is typically inserted into the cavities to reinforce the walls, and then concrete is poured in. Once the concrete cures, the foam remains in place to insulate the walls. Exterior siding and interior wall finishes are attached to the ICFs.

INSULATION
A material that has a high resistance to heat flow. Used to keep a home comfortable and reduce the energy needed to heat and cool the home.

INTEGRATED BUILDING DESIGN
A design process that takes into account the interrelatedness of all parts of a building. It involves designing a building from the outset so that all its components, equipment, and systems work together to provide maximum comfort, healthfulness, energy and resource efficiency, and cost effectiveness.

INVERTER
A device used to convert DC electricity (such as that produced by a photovoltaic system) into AC electricity to power standard household equipment and appliances.

LIGHT STRAW-CLAY CONSTRUCTION
A building method in which loose straw coated with wet clay is tamped into formwork to create insulating, nonstructural walls. The straw-clay mixture can be used as infill between structural members of a framed building or can surround the framed structure.

LIGHTING CONTROLS
Devices used to manually or automatically dim electric lights or switch them on or off. These devices, which include dimmers, timers, motion sensors, and photocell controls, provide convenience and energy savings.

LINOLEUM
A smooth floor covering typically used in kitchens and bathrooms. True linoleum is made from natural renewable resources, including pine rosin, sawdust, linseed oil, natural pigments, and jute. Vinyl flooring, sometimes mistakenly called linoleum, is made from polyvinyl chloride (PVC), which is derived from petrochemicals.

LOAD CALCULATION
Engineering calculations used to determine what size heating and/or cooling system to install in a home, based on the climate, the home's size, type of insulation, amount of glazing, number and orientation of windows, and other factors.

LOW-E (LOW-EMISSIVITY) WINDOW
A window with a special coating that allows daylight to enter a building but reduces the flow of heat. The appropriate type of low-e glazing for a home will depend on the climate and the window's orientation.

MIXED-USE DEVELOPMENT
A building or site that combines several types of commercial uses (retail, office, restaurants, etc.) with housing, rather than segregating commercial and residential uses into separate zones or neighborhoods.

NATIONAL FENESTRATION RATING COUNCIL (NFRC)
An industry organization in the United States that promotes a voluntary energy rating system for windows, skylights, and doors. The NFRC label rates how well a window keeps heat inside a building, the window's ability to block heat from the sun, how much light passes through a window, and how much heat is gained or lost due to cracks around the window assembly.

NATIVE VEGETATION
Plants that are indigenous to a particular area, as opposed to occurring there due to human intervention.

NATURAL COOLING
Cooling a building through passive means rather than using mechanical systems such as air conditioning. Natural cooling strategies include shading, cross ventilation, and the use of thermal mass to moderate temperatures inside a space.

NATURAL VENTILATION
The process of supplying air to and removing air from the interior of a building by using passive means such as open windows and cross-ventilation, rather than using mechanical systems such as air conditioners or heating systems.

NET METERING
A billing agreement available in many states that allows small power producers, such as homeowners with photovoltaic systems, to feed directly to the utility grid any electricity they generate in excess of their current demand. This causes the electricity meter to spin backwards. The homeowner is billed only for the *net* amount of electricity used annually (total electricity used minus total electricity produced by the PV system).

NEW URBANISM
A community planning movement that has evolved as an antidote to the sprawling, automobile-centric suburbs that have dominated U.S. development for the past fifty years. New Urbanists advocate revitalizing older cities and building new communities that feature safe, walkable neighborhoods; a balance of housing and jobs; well-planned open and public spaces; a diversity of housing types; access to public transit; and regionally appropriate architecture.

NFRC
See National Fenestration Rating Council.

NONRENEWABLE RESOURCE
A natural resource that does not replenish itself or is consumed at a faster rate than it is replaced in the environment. Primarily refers to oil, minerals, gas, and coal.

NONTOXIC
Not posing a significant risk to people or the environment.

OFFGAS
The release of vapors from a material through the process of evaporation or chemical decomposition. Many building products, furnishings, floor and wall coverings, and other products brought into the home offgas formaldehyde, volatile organic compounds (VOCs), or other potentially troublesome chemicals.

OLD-GROWTH TREE
A tree that has been growing for approximately 200 years or longer.

ORGANIC GARDENING
Gardening without synthetic pesticides, herbicides, or fertilizers, instead using environmentally responsible techniques and substances like compost, mulch, and manure to build healthy soils, manage pests, and encourage healthy plant growth.

ORIENTATION
The relationship of a building, or a window or other building component, to compass direction and consequently to the sun's position.

ORIENTED STRAND BOARD
An engineered wood panel made from strands of wood arranged in crisscrossing layers and bound with an adhesive.

PARALLEL STRAND LUMBER
An engineered wood product made from strands of wood glued together under pressure and cut to form beams, columns, and other structural building components.

PARTICULATE
Very fine particles in the air, such as smoke, dust, soot, or pollen.

PASSIVE SOLAR DESIGN
A building specifically designed to collect and store the sun's heat, then release that heat into the interior spaces to help warm the rooms naturally. Depending on the design and climate, passive solar heating can be the sole source of heat for the building or can be supplemented with a heating system.

PEDESTRIAN SCALE
A neighborhood design that encourages walking by providing safe streets, which are convenient, pleasant and visually interesting, and that connect to the places people want to get to.

PHANTOM LOAD
The small amounts of electricity consumed by many appliances and equipment—such as TVs and stereos with remotes, ovens with digital clocks, cell phone chargers, and answering machines—even when they're not in use.

PHOTOCELL CONTROL
A device that automatically turns electric lights on or off depending on daylight levels. In homes, photocell controls are usually used to automatically turn on outdoor lights at dusk and turn them off at dawn.

PHOTOVOLTAIC (PV) CELL
A material that converts sunlight directly into electricity.

POLYVINYL CHLORIDE
Also known as vinyl or PVC. A family of plastics, derived from vinyl chloride, with a wide range of forms and uses. PVC is used extensively in building products, consumer goods, and industrial applications. There has been considerable debate about the environmental impacts related to PVC manufacturing and the eventual disposal of products made from PVC. Some groups have called for phasing out PVC production or limiting its use.

POST-CONSUMER RECYCLED CONTENT
Products that have been used and discarded by a consumer and are then reprocessed as raw material for a new product.

PROGRAMMABLE THERMOSTAT
A thermostat that controls a heating and/or cooling system according to the resident's schedule. It allows the resident to preset different temperatures for different times of the day, and with some products, different days of the week.

PUMICECRETE CONSTRUCTION
A type of concrete construction that uses a low-density concrete mix made of portland cement, water, and pumice aggregate (the pumice replaces the sand and gravel that's typically in concrete).

PVC
See polyvinyl chloride.

RADIANT BARRIER
A material installed in buildings to reduce summer heat gain (and, to a lesser extent, winter heat loss). Radiant barrier products typically consist of a thin sheet of a reflective material such as aluminum attached to a substrate such as plywood, oriented strand board, or kraft paper. The product is typically installed in a home's attic to reduce the transfer of heat from the roof into the home.

RADIATION
The transfer of heat from a warm object to a cooler object by means of electromagnetic waves passing through air or space. When you stand in the sun, your skin is warmed by radiation. When you stand next to a cold window, your body radiates heat to the cooler window.

RADON
A radioactive gas derived from the natural decay of uranium. Radon is emitted by some soils and rocks, and can enter a home through cracks and holes in the foundation or through well water.

RAINWATER HARVESTING
Collecting rainwater from a catchment area such as a roof and storing it in cisterns or other containers to use for watering a yard or garden, or for other purposes.

RAMMED-EARTH CONSTRUCTION
Buildings, walls, or other structures made from a moist mix of earth, sand, and cement tamped or "rammed" into temporary forms. The compressed earthen walls cure to a rock-like hardness.

RECLAIMED MATERIAL
A material that's put to a new beneficial use after it's no longer needed for its original use, such as

wood removed from an abandoned building and used to construct a new building.

RECYCLING
Taking a material that would otherwise become waste and processing it into raw material used to make a new product.

RENEWABLE ENERGY
Energy generated from replenishable resources, such as sunlight, wind, and agricultural products.

RENEWABLE RESOURCE
A material that can be replenished in a relatively short period of time after it is harvested or used.

R-VALUE
A measure of a material's resistance to the passage of heat through it. The higher the R-value, the more effective the material is as insulation.

SEALED-COMBUSTION GAS FIREPLACE
A gas-burning fireplace with a sealed combustion chamber. It reduces infiltration because fresh air is supplied directly to the combustion chamber from outside instead of being drawn from inside the room. Harmful combustion by-products are kept out of the home because the combustion exhaust vents directly to the outside.

SEER
Seasonal Energy Efficiency Ratio. Indicates an air conditioner's energy efficiency. The higher the SEER, the more efficient the air conditioner.

SKYLIGHT
A translucent or transparent window set into a roof to allow daylight into a building.

SMART GROWTH
A community planning movement that offers an alternative to unchecked, sprawling development. It advocates protecting open space and farmland, preserving natural and cultural resources, revitalizing inner cities and inner suburbs, and creating communities that are livable and affordable.

SOLAR COLLECTOR
A device used to capture solar energy to heat water.

SOLAR HEAT GAIN COEFFICIENT (SHGC)
An indication of how much of the sun's heat will enter through a window. An SHGC of 0.40, for example, means that 40 percent of the sun's heat passes through the window.

SOLAR ELECTRICITY
Electricity generated from sunlight. Also called photovoltaic or PV electricity.

SPECTRALLY SELECTIVE GLASS

Window glass that has been treated with a special coating or tint that allows visible light to pass into the home, but that blocks much of the sun's heat from entering through the window.

SPRAWL

The spread of low-density, dispersed residential and commercial development outside of compact cities, towns, and villages.

SPRAYED-EARTH CONSTRUCTION

Erecting walls using a high-pressure hose to spray a moist mix of earth, sand, and cement against one-sided formwork.

STEEL FRAMING

Constructing a building shell using steel studs, steel joists, and other steel components instead of wood.

STORM WATER RUNOFF

Water that flows off of buildings and paved surfaces and over land during a rainstorm.

STRAW BALE CONSTRUCTION

A construction method that uses straw bales to form walls. The bales can be load-bearing, meaning that they carry some or all of the roof's weight. More commonly, however, the bales are stacked within a structural framework to provide superior insulation. Straw is an agricultural waste product—it's what's left after harvesting rice, wheat, barley, and other grains.

STRUCTURAL INSULATING PANEL (SIP)

An alternative to framing with wood studs and joists. SIPs can be used to build well-insulated floors, walls, and roofs. They are prefabricated panels that typically consist of rigid foam insulation sandwiched between two panels of oriented strand board or plywood.

SUSTAINABILITY

Meeting the needs of the present without compromising the ability of future generations to meet their own needs (as defined by the World Commission on the Environment and Development).

SWALE

A shallow depression or hollow in the ground used to slow the flow of storm water off a property.

TANKLESS WATER HEATER

See demand water heater.

THERMAL BRIDGE

A highly conductive material within a building envelope, such as a steel framing member, that allows heat to bypass the insulation.

THERMAL MASS

The ability of a material to absorb and retain heat. Materials with high thermal mass, such as rocks, earth, and concrete, have the capacity to absorb heat during the day and release it when the air temperature cools.

TOXIC

Capable of adversely affecting organisms.

TRANSIT-ORIENTED DEVELOPMENT (TOD)

A community where homes, workplaces, schools, neighborhood services, and recreational areas are located in close walking proximity to transit stops, making it convenient for people to work, live, and play without relying excessively on cars.

TRUSS

A prefabricated, structural framework for supporting roofs or floors. Trusses, which are shipped to the building site ready to install, are typically fashioned of small pieces of wood joined with metal plates into a triangulated form. They use less wood, and save time and money compared to site-built rafters and joists.

TRUTH WINDOW

An opening in a wall surface that reveals the components within the wall.

TUBULAR SKYLIGHT

A circular skylight that's much smaller than typical skylights, designed to illuminate interiors with daylight while keeping out excessive heat. It consists of a small, roof-mounted dome attached to a tube lined with reflective material. Light is reflected down the tube and is transmitted into the room through a translucent ceiling fixture.

U-FACTOR

Indicates how easily heat will pass through a construction assembly, such as a window. The lower the U-factor, the lower the rate of heat flow.

UNCONDITIONED SPACE

A space that is neither directly nor indirectly heated or cooled by a home's mechanical systems (for example, a garage or crawlspace).

UNIVERSAL DESIGN

An approach to designing a product or a building to make it more easily usable by people of all ages and diverse physical abilities.

UTILITY GRID

The network of transmission and distribution lines that provides electricity to the vast majority of homes and buildings in the United States and Canada.

VENTILATION

The process of supplying air to and removing from air from an indoor space by natural or mechanical means.

VINYL

See polyvinyl chloride.

VISIBLE TRANSMITTANCE

Indicates the percentage of visible light transmitted through a window. The higher the visible transmittance, the more light is transmitted.

VOLATILE ORGANIC COMPOUND (VOC)

A class of organic chemicals that readily release vapors at room temperature. VOCs occur naturally in many materials, and can also be manufactured and added to materials and products. VOCs are released ("offgassed") into a home by common furnishings and building materials, including many types of particleboard, paint, solvents, carpets, and synthetic fabrics. Exposure to VOCs can cause symptoms ranging from short-term nausea, eye irritation, and headaches to more severe, longer-lasting effects.

WHOLE-HOUSE FAN

A powerful fan mounted in a ceiling opening, used to pull air through the home and exhaust it out the attic and through the roof vents. It provides air circulation and cooling in climates where days are warm and nights are cooler, and can often reduce or eliminate the need for air conditioning. A whole-house fan is typically used at night to pull cooler outside air into the home through open windows, and to vent warm air through the attic and roof.

WOOD-EFFICIENT FRAMING

See advanced wood framing.

XERISCAPE

Landscaping design that conserves water by using native or drought-tolerant plants, mulch, and limited or no irrigation.

GREEN BUILDING

BOOKS

The Art of Natural Building. Joseph F. Kennedy, Michael G. Smith, and Catherine Wanek, editors. Gabriola Island, BC: New Society Publishers, 2002.
Thorough introduction to natural building—straw bale, rammed earth, cob, and more. Includes sections on design and planning as well as building materials and techniques.

The Beauty of Straw Bale Homes. Athena Swentzell Steen and Bill Steen. White River Junction, VT: Chelsea Green Publishing Company, 2001.
Small book with beautiful photographs of straw bale homes. An excellent companion to the Steens' earlier book, The Straw Bale House.

Building with Vision: Optimizing and Finding Alternatives to Wood. Dan Imhoff. Healdsburg, CA: Watershed Media, 2001.
Guide to using wood wisely and using alternatives to wood. Includes lists of resources and suppliers.

Efficient Wood Use in Residential Construction. Ann Edminster and Sami Yassa. New York: Natural Resources Defense Council, 1998.
Available from www.nrdc.org. Guidelines for using wood wisely in home building, with sections on prefabricated components, advanced framing techniques, certified and reclaimed wood, and construction-site waste reduction.

Green Architecture. James Wines. Koln, Germany: Taschen, 2000.
Analysis of contemporary ecological architecture with an emphasis on commercial buildings.

The Natural House. Daniel D. Chiras. White River Junction, VT: Chelsea Green Publishing Company, 2000.
Focus on natural building methods, including straw bale, rammed earth, cob, and adobe. Includes chapters on achieving energy independence with passive solar systems and electricity generation.

The New Natural House Book. David Pearson. New York: Fireside, 1998.
Room-by-room ecological design guide focusing on health and spirit.

The Rammed Earth House. David Easton. White River Junction, VT: Chelsea Green Publishing Company, 1996.
Comprehensive exploration of the history and process of rammed-earth construction.

The Straw Bale House. Athena Swentzell Steen, Bill Steen, David Bainbridge, and David Eisenberg. White River Junction, VT: Chelsea Green Publishing Company, 1994.
Detailed guide to building homes with straw bales.

PERIODICALS

Environmental Building News, www.buildinggreen.com. Brattleboro, VT: Building Green.
Monthly newsletter featuring comprehensive technical information on sustainable building, with a focus on commercial buildings.

The Last Straw, www.strawhomes.com. Hillsboro, NM: The Last Straw.
Quarterly journal about news and developments in the world of straw bale building.

Natural Home, www.naturalhomemagazine.com. Loveland, CO: Natural Home Magazine.
Bimonthly magazine featuring sustainable homes, decorating tips, and information on green products and services.

ENERGY EFFICIENCY and RENEWABLE ENERGY

BOOKS

Consumer Guide to Home Energy Savings. American Council for an Energy-Efficient Economy, Washington, DC
The Most Energy-Efficient Appliances. American Council for an Energy-Efficient Economy, Washington, DC
Available from www.aceee.org.
Regularly updated booklets with information on the most energy-efficient appliances sold in the United States.

EEBA Builder's Guides. Joe Lstiburek and Betsy Pettit. Bloomington, MN: Energy and Environmental Building Association, 2000–2002.
Available from www.eeba.org.
Series of technical manuals on how to build energy- and resource-efficient homes in four climate zones: cold, mixed/humid, hot/dry, and hot/humid.

Energy-Efficient Building: The Best of Fine Homebuilding. Newtown, CT: Taunton Press, 1999.
Collection of 29 articles from Fine Homebuilding magazine, with techniques for making your home more energy efficient and comfortable.

Real Goods Solar Living Source Book. John Schaeffer and Doug Pratt, editors. Hopland, CA: Gaiam Real Goods, 2001.
Comprehensive guide to renewable energy technologies, from the company that provides renewable energy products and products for sustainable living.

The Solar House: Passive Heating and Cooling. Daniel D. Chiras. White River Junction, VT: Chelsea Green Publishing Company, 2002.
From the author of The Natural House.
Comprehensive information on using sunlight, natural ventilation, and appropriate design to passively heat and cool houses.

PERIODICALS

Home Energy, www.homeenergy.org. Berkeley, CA: Home Energy Magazine.
Bimonthly magazine providing information on home energy conservation, indoor air quality, and other green building topics.

Solar Today, www.solartoday.org. Boulder, CO: Solar Today Magazine.
Bi-monthly magazine that covers all solar technologies.

WEBSITES

www.ase.org/consumer. Alliance to Save Energy, Washington, DC
User-friendly Website with tips for consumers on how to cut energy use, increase comfort, and save money.

www.efficientwindows.org. Efficient Windows Collaborative, Washington, DC
Information on the benefits of energy-efficient windows, with tips for selecting the right windows for your home.

www.energystar.gov. Energy Star program, U.S. Environmental Protection Agency and U.S. Department of Energy, Washington, DC
Program sponsored by the U.S. government to promote energy-efficient homes and household products. Website provides useful articles, links, and lists of Energy Star–labeled products and homes.

www.eere.energy.gov/buildings/homes. Energy Efficiency and Renewable Energy Network (EREN), U.S. Department of Energy, Washington, DC
Comprehensive Website providing information on efficient heating and cooling, water conservation, passive solar design, photovoltaics, energy-efficient remodeling. Also includes energy-efficiency tips for renters.

www.eere.energy.gov/power/consumer. Consumer Guide to Renewable Energy, U.S. Department of Energy, Washington, DC
Information on generating your own electricity, including a state-by-state listing of renewable energy resources and financial incentives.

http://oee.nrcan.gc.ca/publications. Office of Energy Efficiency, Natural Resources Canada, Ottawa, ON
Series of articles and fact sheets on energy-efficient home building and home renovations for Canadian consumers.

www.rmi.org. Rocky Mountain Institute, Snowmass, CO
Nonprofit organization that provides helpful tips and fact sheets on home energy efficiency, appliances and lighting, water efficiency, indoor air quality, and more.

HEALTHY HOME/INDOOR AIR QUALITY

BOOKS

Prescriptions for a Healthy House: A Practical Guide for Architects, Builders, and Homeowners. Paula Baker-Laporte, Erica Elliott, and John Banta. Gabriola Island, BC: New Society Publishers, 2001. *Resource guide for designing and building a healthy and resource-efficient home. Focuses on indoor air quality and health issues. Includes extensive product recommendations.*

WEBSITES

www.epa.gov/iaq. U.S. Environmental Protection Agency, Washington, DC
Information on various indoor air-quality topics, including asthma, mold, radon, and more. Provides extensive links to other indoor air-quality Websites, and a toll-free hotline for indoor air-quality questions.

www.lungusa.org/air/air_indoor_index.html. American Lung Association, New York, NY
General information on the sources and effects of indoor air pollution, and tips for improving air quality in your home.

GREEN PRODUCTS

BOOKS

Cradle to Cradle: Remaking the Way We Make Things. William McDonough and Michael Braungart. New York: North Point Press, 2002.
Presents a vision for a new industrial paradigm in which products are designed not just to do less harm, but to do good for the world.

EcoDesign: The Sourcebook. Alastair Fuad-Luke. San Francisco: Chronicle Books, 2002.
Resource guide to hundreds of innovative, environmentally responsible products, from building materials and furniture to cars and clothing.

WEBSITES

www.certifiedwood.org. Forest Certification Resource Center, Certified Forest Products Council, Portland, OR
Searchable on-line database of FSC-certified products.

www.environmentalhomecenter.com. Environmental Home Center, Seattle, WA
National distributor of green building supplies and household products.

COMMUNITY PLANNING

BOOKS

Suburban Nation: The Rise of Sprawl and the Decline of the American Dream. Andres Duany, Elizabeth Plater-Zyberk, and Jeff Speck. New York: North Point Press, 2000.
Examines what went wrong with urban and suburban development in the post–World War II years, and what we can do to revitalize our cities and suburbs.

WEBSITES

www.cnu.org. Congress for the New Urbanism, San Francisco, CA
Nonprofit organization that promotes New Urbanism. Website lists many New Urbanist communities in the United States and Canada.

GENERAL HOME DESIGN

BOOKS

The Not So Big House. Sarah Susanka and Kira Obolensky. Newton, CT: Taunton Press, 2001. *Influential book about creating smaller homes that put quality above quantity.*

Patterns of Home: The Ten Essentials of Enduring Design. Max Jacobson, Murray Silverstein, and Barbara Winslow. Newtown, CT: Taunton Press, 2002. *Covers fundamental aspects of home design, from creating a home that's in tune with the surrounding environment to making the most of the sun's light and warmth.*

WEBSITES

www.aarp.org/universalhome. Universal Design Home Modification, AARP, Washington, DC
Helpful tips for creating homes that are usable by people of all ages and physical abilities.

PROJECT CREDITS

All photographs copyright Linda Svendsen, except where otherwise noted.

Backcover, pp. 8, 37, 128–133. **ARCHITECT: ARKIN TILT ARCHITECTS**, Albany, CA, Tel. 510/528.9830, www.arkintilt.com.

pp. 10, 34–35, 98. **DEVELOPER/BUILDER: TERRAFIRMA BUILDING**, Portland, OR, Tel. 503/282.2271, www.terrafirmabldg.com.

pp. 13, 17, 57. **ARCHITECT: LIVING SHELTER DESIGN**, Issaquah, WA, Tel. 425/427.8643, www.livingshelter.com.

pp. 14, 16, 65, 125–127, 141. **DESIGNER/BUILDER: RAMMED EARTH DEVELOPMENT**, Tucson, AZ, Tel. 520/623.2784, www.rammedearth.com.

p. 18. Dewees Island, SC. Tel. 843/886.8783, www.deweesisland.com. Photos courtesy Dewees Island.

pp. 19 (bottom), 30–32, 82, 109 (top), 137 (left), 139, 140 (left). **DEVELOPER/BUILDER: PARDEE HOMES**, San Diego, CA, Tel. 858/621.5888, www.pardeehomes.com.

p. 20. **DEVELOPER/OWNER: BELMONT LIMITED PARTNERSHIP; PROJECT MANAGER: SHIELS OBLETZ JOHNSEN, INC.**, Portland, OR, Tel. 503/242.0084, www.sojpdx.com; **ARCHITECT: GBD ARCHITECTS, INC.**, Portland, OR, Tel. 503/224.9656, www.gbdarchitects.com.

pp. 20–21 (center). **DEVELOPER/OWNER: ALDER STREET HOLDINGS, LLC; PROJECT MANAGER: SHIELS OBLETZ JOHNSEN, INC.**, Portland, OR, Tel. 503/242.0084, www.sojpdx.com; **ARCHITECT: GBD ARCHITECTS, INC.**, Portland, OR, Tel. 503/224.9656, www.gbdarchitects.com.

p. 21 (top right and middle right). **DEVELOPER: HOLT & HAUGH COMPANIES**, Portland, OR, Tel. 503/222-5522, www.fairviewvillage.com.

p. 21 (bottom right). **DEVELOPER: SOCKEYE DEVELOPMENT, LLC; PROJECT MANAGER: SHIELS OBLETZ JOHNSEN, INC.**, Portland, OR, Tel. 503/242.0084, www.sojpdx.com; **ARCHITECT: THOMAS HACKER ARCHITECTS, INC.**, Portland, OR, Tel. 503/227.1254, www.thomashacker.com.

pp. 23, 78, 99. **ARCHITECT/BUILDER: TODD JERSEY ARCHITECTURE**, Berkeley, CA, Tel. 510/524-5666, www.toddjerseyarchitecture.com.

pp. 22, 90–91. **DESIGNER/BUILDER: NEIL KELLY DESIGNERS/REMODELERS**, Portland, OR, Tel. 503/288.7461, www.neilkelly.com.

pp. 26–29, 109 (bottom), 113–117, 137 (right). **ARCHITECT/BUILDER: LEGER WANASELJA ARCHITECTURE**, Berkeley, CA, Tel. 510/848.8901, www.lwarc.com.

p. 36. Dewees Island, SC. Tel. 843/886.8783, www.deweesisland.com. Photo © Rick Rhodes.

Front cover, pp. 39–41. **ARCHITECT: ALLISON EWING AND CHRISTOPHER HAYS**, Charlottesville, VA, Tel. 434/979.1494. **BUILDER: CRAIG DUBOSE**, Charlottesville, VA. Photos © Prakash Patel.

pp. 43, 67–71. **ARCHITECT: DAVID HERTZ/SYNDESIS, INC.**, Santa Monica, CA, Tel. 310/829.9932, www.syndesisinc.com.

pp. 45, 50–53, 151. **DEVELOPER: MICHAEL MCKEEL**, Gresham, OR, Tel. 503/663.3829. **ARCHITECT: ROSS CHAPIN ARCHITECTS**, Langley, WA, 360/221.2373, www.rosschapin.com.

pp. 46–49. **ARCHITECT: DON GURNEY ARCHITECT, INC.**, West Vancouver, British Columbia, Tel. 604/926.7501, **BUILDER: HART TIPTON CONSTRUCTION**, Vancouver, British Columbia.

pp. 54, 60, 79–81. **ARCHITECT: EHDD ARCHITECTURE**, San Francisco, CA, Tel. 415/285.9193, www.ehdd.com. **DESIGNER/GREEN BUILDING CONSULTANT: SANDRA SLATER ENVIRONMENTS**, Palo Alto, CA, Tel. 650/566.0550, www.sandraslater.com. **BUILDER: DREW MARAN CONSTRUCTION/DESIGN**, Palo Alto, CA, Tel. 650/323.8541, www.drewmaran.com.

pp. 58–59, 89. **ARCHITECT: DAVID HERTZ/SYNDESIS, INC.**, Santa Monica, CA, Tel. 310/829.9932, www.syndesisinc.com. **DESIGNER/BUILDER: DESMOND B. AND JULIE MCDONALD**, Los Angeles, CA, Tel. 310/466.6164; Mark Sansone.

pp. 61 (top), 74, 83, 106. **Community of Civano**, Tucson, AZ, Tel. 520/298.8900, www.civano.com.

COMMUNITY DESIGN AND PLANNING: DUANY PLATER-ZYBERK & COMPANY ARCHITECTS AND TOWN PLANNERS, Miami, FL, Tel. 305/644.1023, www.dpz.com; **MOULE + POLYZOIDES ARCHITECTS AND URBANISTS**, Pasadena, CA, 626/844.2400, www.mparchitects.com. **BUILDERS: CONTRAVEST, DOUCETTE HOMES, SOLARBUILT, AND TJ BEDNAR HOMES.**

pp. 61 (bottom), 73, 86–88, 135, 140 (right). **GREEN BUILDING CONSULTANT: O'BRIEN & CO.**, Bainbridge Island, WA, Tel. 206/842.8995, www.obrienandco.com. **ARCHITECT: ASPECTS ARCHITECTURAL SERVICES, INC.**, Lake Forest Park, WA, Tel. 206/363.8805. **BUILDER: WOODSIDE CONSTRUCTION, INC.**, Kingston, WA, Tel. 360/297.4543.

pp. 84–85. **OWNER/DEVELOPER: COMMUNITY CORP. OF SANTA MONICA**, Tel. 310/394.8487. **ARCHITECT: PUGH SCARPA KODAMA**, Santa Monica, CA, Tel. 310/828.0226, www.pugh-scarpa.com. **PROJECT FUNDERS: CITY OF SANTA MONICA; CALIFORNIA DEPARTMENT OF HOUSING AND COMMUNITY DEVELOPMENT**; additional funding provided through grants, rebates, and a coalition of local utility and government agencies.

pp. 92–95. **ARCHITECT: STEVE BADANES**, University of Washington, Seattle, WA, Tel. 206/543.7144.

pp. 96, 102–105. **Owner designed and built.**

p. 110. **ARCHITECT: SIEGEL & STRAIN ARCHITECTS**, Emeryville, CA, Tel. 510/547.8092, www.siegelstrain.com. **DEVELOPERS: CITY OF EMERYVILLE REDEVELOPMENT AGENCY; ALAMEDA COUNTY SOURCE REDUCTION AND RECYCLING BOARD.**

pp. 119–123, 134. **ARCHITECT: VAN DER RYN ARCHITECTS**, Sausalito, CA, Tel. 415/332.5806, www.vanderryn.com.

pp. 142–145. **DESIGNER/BUILDER: GRANT BROSIUS**, Topanga Canyon, CA, Tel. 310/455.0582.

pp. 146–149. **ARCHITECT: SALAL ARCHITECTURE**, Bowen Island, British Columbia, Tel. 604/947.0537. **BUILDER: ELAHO DESIGN & BUILD**, East Vancouver, British Columbia, Tel. 604/321.7312.

ACKNOWLEDGMENTS

Many thanks to the homeowners who opened their doors and warmly shared a part of their lives with me. This book couldn't have happened without them. Thanks, too, to the talented architects, builders, designers, and green building advocates who have been so generous with their time and expertise. I'd also like to acknowledge all the people who pointed me toward hundreds of good green homes around the country and around the world—coming up with a short list of homes to feature in this book was a bittersweet task because it meant leaving out so many wonderful places.

I'm deeply grateful to many colleagues and friends for their enthusiasm, thoughtful insights, and careful critiques of my manuscript, especially Charles Eley, Beth Gerber, Chris Hammer, Cathy Higgins, Diane Horner, Karen King, Erik Kolderup, Larry Mayers, and Geof Syphers. If, despite their fine efforts, any gaffes appear in these pages, the fault lies entirely with me. Thanks too, to Linda Svendsen, whose spirit is as beautiful as her photography, to Dawn DeVries Sokol who created such an appealing design, and to Suzanne Taylor and the rest of the Gibbs Smith team who worked so hard to bring this book into being.

And mostly, I'm grateful to Erik, for his unswerving love and support, and for now and then prompting me to set work aside and go for a long motorcycle ride.